Raised bed

A beginners guide to build your own raised bed garden even if you are a complete beginner. How to plant and take care of your own stuff even at home.

Introduction Of Gardening

Traditional gardeners have been making use of raised beds to grow their vegetables for many years. They would double dig the beds, creating circular or rectangular mounds a foot or so high with the sloping edges on the sides of the beds. This is especially effective in areas that receive lots of rain since it guarantees good drainage. Additionally, it allows a bit more space to grow your veggies.

Companion planting works perfectly on raised beds. Those vegetables which need more space for their roots like carrots would be planted on top while others like leeks and onions would fill up the space on the sides of your beds. The latter repels pests and would act as a shield for the carrot plants on the top of the bed.

These are but a few of the numerous benefits of gardening in raised beds. Therefore, it is not surprising to find that our modern-day gardeners are turning their attention with more frequency to this method. They have added a twist though, now solid frames replace these sloping sides to give the raised beds a distinct and well-defined structure. What this means is that you can make the beds as high or tall as you want them to be without the danger of soil runoff when it rains.

It might sound like a huge job, but these modern raised gardening beds are easy to assemble or build by yourself. Frames can be built with concrete blocks, timber or bricks and then filled with many organic materials mixed with soil. You will find kits ready for assembling as well as prefabricated plastic containers at almost any gardening center. Now anyone and everyone can easily and successfully grow their vegetables in raised beds.

One of the most popular styles of gardening today is raised gardening. Why is this type of gardening so popular? Why do people prefer it to regular gardening or container gardening, which is relatively simpler to set up and easier to maintain? Why are so many eBooks on raised bed gardening becoming bestsellers overnight? There are many, many advantages that one can enjoy with this type of gardening. Here are 13 of the top quoted reasons:

Raised bed gardening is great for small areas of land.

You can plant more because you do not need to worry about having a path in between the plants for walking.

You do not have many about which weeds to worry.

It is easier to keep pests away – especially slugs and snails.

It is a great option for places that are drought-affected/ have water scarcity.

Raised gardens can be built to suit any height needed. It is easy to garden for people who cannot bend, are confined to wheelchairs or have any other type of physical challenges.

Raised gardens require little to no maintenance.

Raised gardens make it easy to adapt the square foot gardening method. Square foot gardening is when you divide the garden into one square foot plot.

You do not need much digging once the garden is set up for the earth is compact and well aired.

The raised bed can be made into any shape – as per your desire and/or need.

You can have different types of soil for different beds. For example, you can have rich soil for pumpkins, sandy soil for carrots, and so on. You can also easily rotate your plants/flowers in any way that suits you.

You have the best drainage with this type of gardening. This is of immense help if you live in an area where the soil is waterlogged. You will not have to worry about root rot.

You can bid goodbye to gophers or any other burrowing pests as you can "close" the bottom of your raised garden with wire mesh (like you use in chicken coops) to prevent any pest from burrowing into your garden from underneath.

Why It Is Suitable For You

Companion planting works perfectly in raised beds. Those vegetables which need more space for their roots like carrots should be planted on top while others like leeks and onions will fill up the space on the sides of your beds. The leeks and onions repel pests and will act as a shield for the carrot plants on the top of the bed.

These are but a few of the numerous benefits of gardening in raised beds. Therefore, it is not surprising to find that our modern-day gardeners are turning their attention with more frequency to this method. They have added a twist, though; now solid frames replace these sloping sides to give the raised beds a distinct and well-defined structure. What this means is that you can make the beds as high or tall as you want them to be without the danger of soil runoff when it rains.

It might sound like a huge job, but these modern raised gardening beds are easy to assemble or build by yourself. Frames can be built with concrete blocks, timber, or bricks and then filled with many organic materials mixed with soil. You will find kits ready for assembling as well as prefabricated plastic containers at almost any gardening center. Now anyone and everyone can easily and successfully grow their vegetables in raised beds and enjoy their own fresh produce.

Benefits of Raised Bed Gardening Method

1.   Excellent Aeration

The older, traditional way to create raised beds is simply to dig up the soil, piling it into rows. You can follow this method and then support the two sides by using solid frames. Otherwise, place your frames in place and then fill them up with compost, farmyard manure mixed with quality soil. Whichever way you choose to do it, your plants will flourish in this enriched soil, and its loose structure will allow excellent air circulation around all the roots.

We know that the different parts of plants all need to breathe, and so do the roots. For example, during photosynthesis, the leaves take in carbon dioxide and expel oxygen. If your plant sits in compact soil, the roots will suffocate and will not succeed in developing fully. This is because they need good aeration for their roots to be able to absorb the essential nutrients in the soil. To explain further, the soil bacteria convert the nitrogen in the little air pockets into nitrate salts and nitrate, thus providing the macronutrients for the plant. Without sufficient air, there is a lack of nitrogen, and therefore less nutrients will be available to the plant.

It is clear that the population of microbes in your vegetable soil must be kept healthy, and this is made possible with well aerated soil. The balance of anaerobic and aerobic bacteria should be maintained as they all play their different roles to enhance the fertility of the soil.

2.   Good Drainage

Even during a downpour of rain, your raised beds will render good drainage. No wonder this method is so popular in the tropics with its heavy rainfall. Because the soil has such a loose texture, water will seep slowly into the bed instead of a making a quick runoff with the accompanying washing away of all fertile topsoil. Furthermore, all the excess water can easily drain away.

Although most plants do not mind moisture at all, they hate to get their feet wet. Firstly, all that water around their roots will make breathing almost impossible. Secondly, too much moisture will promote fungal and bacterial diseases. Lastly, excess water drenching the soil can change its pH level and raise the acidity. Plants that prefer more neutral or slightly alkaline soil will suffer as a result.

Some plants, for example, those that live in bogs, are adapted to grow in drenched soil, but most plants prefer soil with a twenty-five percent-moisture level. Raised beds will not allow water stagnation while at the same time, they keep your soil quite evenly moist because the water soaks into the lowest levels of your beds quickly.

3.   The Spreading of Roots

Although plant roots can be quite persistent in their effort to grow, they will find it difficult to do so in tightly compacted soil. In loose soil they can grow and spread out to their hearts' content. Furthermore, a framed bed will retain the moisture after watering a lot longer than the more traditionally raised beds because the frames prevent water loss on the sides of the beds more effectively. Drying out of the beds can, therefore, be prevented and good root spreading will follow.

Plants growing in non-raised garden beds generally have a very shallow system of roots since they find it impossible to penetrate through the more compact soil deeper down unless of course, you go to the trouble of tilling the soil deeply before you plant your vegetables. This means that the plant roots are unable to get to the moisture kept in the deeper layers, which in turn may lead to dehydration of the plant when the moisture on the surface evaporates. Well-developed root systems anchor your plants. It also enlarges the potential food source area from which the plant can gather its nutrients and water. Vegetable plants, in particular, need enough of both to encourage vigorous growth and maximum yield during their relatively short growing season.

4.   Minimum Risk of Compact Soil

A raised bed will not completely deter your smaller pets like dogs and cats from digging and rolling around in your gardening soil, but it definitely will keep humans and larger pets or animals at bay. This will prevent the tamping down of the soil. The ideal width for your raised beds is three to four feet, making it easy for you to do your gardening chores such as weeding, harvesting, and fertilizing without having to step onto the beds.

The floods, which sometimes occur after a heavy downpour, can also compact the soil of cultivated fields. Wet soil is heavy and will sink down and fill all the little air pockets. Once the water has evaporated, you will be left with a dense, hard layer that is not very accommodating for the plants. Raised beds allow the water to drain away much quicker, preventing floods to cause soil compaction.

5.   Improved Weed Control

Sick and tired of weeding? A raised bed garden is the answer. In a normal vegetable plot, you will find it hard to get rid of all the frustrating weeds no matter how dedicated you are. They just seem to take over all the time.

When you cultivate the soil for normal vegetable beds, you expose a lot of the weed seeds that have been lying dormant underground shielded from the sun. The exposure to sunlight and extra moisture they receive during irrigation will provide them with the opportunity to start sprouting, just what they have been waiting for. Very quickly, they will feed on the nutrient-rich soil prepared for your vegetable plants and begin to flourish.

You can make use of the option to fill your raised beds with relatively weed-free soil and compost. If a few stray weeds appear, your raised beds with its loose soil will make weeding a breeze. A good tip is to fill up your raised beds with as many plants as will grow in it so that they will suffocate and outgrow any stubborn weeds that may try their luck.

6.   Easier than Amending Existing Soil

Garden soil greatly varies from area to area; sometimes, it is more alkaline and chalky, often it is too acidic, and plants will not thrive without your intervention. Vegetables, in general, like slightly acidic to neutral soil, anything with a pH level of between 5.5 and 7.5. Having said that, there are exceptions. Blueberries and tomatoes, for instance, like more acidic soil while asparagus and broccoli prefer to have their roots in sweeter soil.

The remedy for alkaline soil is to add Sulphur, for acidic soil lime can be added. Sometimes applications have to be repeated a number of times to get the desired effect, but a downpour can undo all your hard work in a flash. It is not a simple, straightforward process to change the intrinsic nature of any type of soil.

If you plan to cultivate different kinds of vegetables, raised beds will give you the option of which soil you choose. On top of that, you can now fill up different raised beds with the type of soil each variety of vegetable prefers. The addition of lots of compost, something most gardeners usually do, makes it easier to sustain the soil's neutrality.

7.   Garden on Top of Existing Turf

You have made the decision to start your own vegetable garden, but the task of having to dig up and clean the existing turf presently growing on the area you have targeted is just too daunting. Do not despair; raised vegetable beds can be built straight on top of your grass without having to dig up any sods.

Mark your area, and then place multiple layers of cardboard and newspaper on the area. Erect your frames and then simply continue to fill them with grass clippings, soil, sand, decomposed farmyard manure, and compost. Plant your seeds or seedlings in this rich mixture, and you have started your garden without too much backbreaking labor.

8.   Avoid Root Run from Larger Plants and Trees

Sometimes you will find that the only available space left in your garden for your vegetables is near a number of well-established trees. These trees have massively huge roots to anchor them to the ground and will devour all the nutrients in the soil, leaving very little for your vegetable plants. You may be able to get rid of some of these invasive roots, but it is an impossible task to get completely rid of them all. Using chemicals to try to kill the roots is not an option because these very same chemicals can harm or even kill your vegetable plants. However, your raised beds will be safe from this problem since tree roots generally grow downwards and will not reach into the raised beds.

9.   More Effective Pest Control

Creepy crawlies are true to their description, they usually enter vegetable patches this way, crawling away until they find food. Encountering an obstacle like a solid frame will definitely deter some of them from crawling up. They may just pick the easier option of continuing along the ground. To protect your plants from soil parasites like nematodes, line your raised beds along the sides and the bottom with plastic. If you fear annoying rodents burrowing their way into your beds, use a netting of wire, placing it at the bases of your beds.

Overall, it will be easier to rid your beds of the various offenders just because they are more accessible. Applying chemical or natural pesticides or picking out invaders by hand is a lot less cumbersome if you do not have to bend down to ground level all the time. Everything, including nasty pests, will be more visible to the eye too. Walking along your raised beds, inspecting your plants regularly, you can quickly detect infestations and deal with them immediately. Remember, the sooner you tackle any pests, the easier it will be to rid your vegetable garden of them.

10.   Extra Available Space

Raised beds in the traditional fashion provide more space for plants growing along the sides of the beds. Although this advantage is not applicable to framed beds, they can provide additional space in another manner. Many of the plants growing along the side edges of the frames will extend over these side edges, leaving more room for other plants on the top surface of the bed. More light will be able to reach the plants as well.

Those varieties of tomatoes that normally will need staking can simply be allowed to grow downwards instead of upwards. Make sure the beds you plant them in are high enough. Strawberries and the vines of sweet potatoes tumbling down the sides of your raised beds will make a very pretty picture in your garden and create a luxurious aspect.

11.   Extended Growing Season

We all know how long it takes the ground to thaw in spring, but raised beds speed up this thawing process. This means that you can start transplanting your seedlings much earlier in the season, giving them a wonderful head start. If the area where you live has a short window period to grow your edibles in the outside garden, this extra time will make a huge difference.

Some vegetables, for instance, onions, need a fairly long season to grow to maturity. Three to four months are needed for onions sets, and if you grow them from the seeds, it will take even longer. Seeds give you a much larger choice as only a few varieties are generally available assets. Making use of this advantage of choice means that you will need more time. Fortunately, onion seedlings like cooler weather, so plant them as soon as the soil in your raised beds has thawed.

Towards the end of the autumn, you can also extend your veggies' growing season; just place a few hoop covers onto your bed frames. This is easily done by installing pipe brackets made of metal from which you can attach or remove the hoop covers when necessary. Custom made covers in plastic or glass can be fitted for your individual raised beds as well.

12.   Intensive Gardening with Higher Yield

It is a fact that a higher yield will be obtained by growing your veggies in raised beds rather on flat ground beds. Attributing factors are the good aeration of the soil and extensive root run, but the main cause is the intensive nature of this kind of gardening. Raised beds allow you to plant a greater variety of different kinds of vegetables closer together than could be done on flat ground.

Because the soil used in these raised beds contains more organic matter and compost, it is rich enough to support quite a number of extra plants, definitely more than usual. The plants will completely fill up the beds as they continue to grow with their foliage touching. The close proximity of the plants will prevent weeds from flourishing too.

13.   Solution for Mobility Challenged Gardeners

Not all gardeners are young, energetic, and healthy people. Many experienced gardeners find it difficult to continue bending down for weeding and tending their vegetable patches as they grow older and experience health challenges. Raised beds can be built or assembled to the exact width or height that will suit every individual. It can even be planned and laid out in a fashion to accommodate wheelchair users and allow them freedom of movement to plant and harvest their vegetables easily.

Even if you do not face any of these challenges, you will find it a relief to see to those vegetable plants that need constant attention if they are raised off the ground. Backbreaking work is never fun and may even cause injuries. Salad vegetables and herbs need frequent harvesting, and popping out into the garden to pick a few herbs for your meal will be a lot easier if you do not have to bend down all the time.

14. Portability

If you find that your vegetable plants are not exposed to enough sunlight in their current spot, you can just move your raised bed without too much effort. Portability is one of the advantages of this method of gardening. Beds with wire bottoms can simply be dragged to a brighter location. Otherwise, dismantle the frames and then reassemble your beds in their new spots. With care, you can move the plants, as well as the soil, contend without any damage.

A very practical solution is to buy raised beds that are ready-made and fitted with casters. They are easily moved around, and if early frost overtakes you, they can even be rolled into your heated garage to save your plants.

There are quite a number of variations on the theme of raised bed gardening like square foot, hay bale, and keyhole gardening. They all assist in making growing your own food less of a challenge and a lot more rewarding, something the modern age gardener appreciates.

Strategies In Maintaining Your Raised Bed Garden

By itself, a raised garden does not necessarily require too much maintenance. With that said, there's no reason why you should simply leave everything up to fate and be lazy with it. There are, in fact, ways in which you can ensure the year-round health and success of your raised gardens—

- Mulch your garden after you have planted your greens or blooms. Use materials such as straw, leaves, wood chips or grass clippings. What this does is help reduce the volume of weeds that will develop in your garden, thus avoiding or minimizing the amount of maintenance weeding that you have to do when you tend to your garden.

- Don't compact the soil. This means not walking on it. The greatest advantage of raised bed gardening is the fact that you are using loose, fertile, aerated soil that provides the ideal base for plants, vegetables and herbs to take root. Avoid compacting the soil by stepping on it.

- Water your garden. Like with any garden, your raised bed of greens, florals, vegetables or herbs will need frequent watering. Use a soaker hose or drip irrigation system. You can install this ahead of time so as to avoid having to constantly tend to your garden.

- Take note of your raised bed's surroundings. Do you have large trees? Is the area prone to weeds? You might want to consider installing a barrier at the bottom of your bed that will prevent your plants' roots from having to contend with large tree roots—not just in terms of space but for soil nutrition as well. Barrier options include store-bought weed barriers from your local gardening shops and stores, a piece of old carpet or even a piece of corrugated cardboard. This, however, may take a bit of work. So if you do not intend to excavate the soil or foresee a certain amount of work that you will not be able to provide, think about moving your raised garden bed elsewhere.

- Top up when you can. Think of your raised bed garden as sort of like a giant container garden. While you have prepped your soil to make it as fertile and as ideal for planting as possible, time will eventually allow the soil to settle and it will eventually deplete. When this happens, it will take its toll on your plants. To avoid this, add 1" or 2" layers of compost on the top part of your soil before you even start planting.

- Keep your soil properly aerated to allow your plants' roots to breathe. Fluff the soil with a garden fork until it is properly mixed—do this by sticking a fork deep into the soil and wiggling it through the soil back and forth. Poke through the soil at 8-12" intervals across the entire bed.

- Protect your style. Whether or not you are gardening, be sure to add a layer of mulch or cover crop over your soil—even at the end of your desired growing season. Weather that is too hot will cause the soil to dry out your plants' roots. Soil exposed to too much cold in harsh winters can cause it to break down and compact.

- Do not underestimate cover crops. Ryegrass, crimson closer and hairy vetch, when planted on raised beds after the end of each planting season, will help reduce erosion and aerate your soil properly.

- Extend your planting season with a little creativity. A low tunnel or a cold frame allows you to protect your plants, herbs and flowers regardless of the weather.

- You might want to try composting right on your raised garden bed. Worm tubes, trench composting and dig and drop composting methods can help enrich your soil without having to turn directly to a compost pile.

- Remember that you are not supposed to compact the soil, so make sure that you work from outside the beds. The biggest advantage of working with raised gardens is that the ideal soil conditions allow for better and more successful plant growth via loose and fluffy soil. Stepping on that will cause the soil to compact and restrict the free growth of roots from the garden.

How to Build a Raised Bed

Now you have your location to build your permanent raised bed, you need to gather all your supplies together and this can be done in an afternoon easily depending on what you construct it out of.

What You Will Need

- Hammer (with suitable weight)

- Tape measure

- Pencil

- Saw (circular or miter)

- Drill or impact drill

- Galvanised screws 3" long

- Wood

Considerations When Choosing Materials

- Durability

- Cost effectiveness

- Toxicity

- Aesthetics

- Environmental impact

- Portability

- Maintenance

- Duration of construction

Choosing what you will construct your raised bed has a number of factors and considerations but ultimately it's your choice to suit your budget and the size of the bed. Reclaimed or recycled materials are popular as they are usually the most affordable; they have a low environmental impact, as they don't require any forestry, manufacture or any long-distance transport. If you check locally on free sites, salvage yards or even the local refuse centre regularly you will certainly find reusable materials to use, you just may need to be patient!

I will elaborate below on the different qualities of wood you can use and how this could affect your plants, but I would urge you to do your own research on the different materials to use and find what works best for you and your plot. When I started making my first raised bed garden I went to my local hardware store and bought some timber and was overwhelmed with the choice! Using untreated or organically treated wood is what I now would recommend to build your raised garden. If the budget stretches to it using a naturally rot-resistant wood such as redwood or cedar is a great option and gives a great aesthetic too. They are extremely durable materials to use, will last 15 years at least depending on your weather conditions.

How To Build (And Well-Maintain) Your Own Garden

Seed

Seed starting is not a requirement, but it offers many benefits. It allows you to experiment with varieties not carried by your local nursery and to control chemical inputs and growing practices. In addition, seed starting makes for a great family project—kids love to watch the progress of seedlings.

One other benefit: Seed starting gives plants with long growing seasons—and impatient gardeners—a head start. In many areas of the United States, starting tomato seeds indoors is necessary to ensure that the plants have time to bear fruit before cold weather rolls back around.

Start your seeds indoors 6 to 8 weeks before the last frost in your area, then plant the seedlings outdoors in the garden after the danger of frost has passed.

To start seedlings, first gather your tools and supplies. You will need:

- Plastic oil pan or bucket

- A good seed starting soil mix (a light and fluffy mix clearly marked for starting seeds)

- Peat pots

- Tray for the pots

- Seeds of choice

- Permanent marker

- Stakes to label the plants

- Vented lid (optional)

- Propagation mat (a heating pad for your plants)

- Adjustable fluorescent lights on a timer

- Liquid 20/20/20 houseplant fertilizer (a balanced blend of nitrogen, phosphorous, and potassium)

1. Add enough soil to the oil pan to fill your peat pots, then add water to make the soil just moist enough to be crumbly when pressed in your hand. No water should come out when you squeeze the soil.

2. Fill your peat pots with the moistened (not wet) soil, then place your pots in the tray. (I recommend peat pots, because they are biodegradable, can be planted directly in your garden, and allow healthy root growth. When planting time comes, pull the bottom off the pot and plant your seedling.)

3. Make a hole in the soil using the tip of your finger. Plant 2 or 3 seeds in each hole to the depth specified on the seed packet. Lightly cover each hole with the soil.

4. Mark your seeds with labels as you go, especially if you are planting two or more varieties of the same plant.

5. Place a vented lid over the tray. Keep the vent open until the seedlings appear, then remove the lid. This (and only this) step is optional. Some people cover their trays with plastic wrap or use a spray bottle to keep the soil moist.

6. Place the tray on a propagation mat and plug it in. The mat will raise the soil temperature to assist germination. You can put the tray on the top of your refrigerator, which is warm, but I prefer to keep mine at eye level so I can regularly monitor the seedlings' progress.

7. Once the seedlings sprout, place fluorescent lights directly above the tray, as close as 2 to 4 inches away from the seedling tops. Raise the lights as the plants grow. (Without sufficient light, your plants will become yellow and spindly.)

8. The first "leaves" to appear are the cotyledons; they are actually part of the seed. When the first set of true leaves appears, start fertilizing. (If your soil mix contains fertilizer, skip this step.) Use about a quarter of the amount of fertilizer recommended on the fertilizer bag label, but before you apply the fertilizer, dilute it—and make it half the strength specified on the label.

Many seeds, if stored in a cool, dry, and dark place, could be viable for as many as 5 years, but some seeds are viable for shorter or longer times. Before you plant seeds of suspect viability, do a germination test to determine whether they will sprout. Place 10 seeds on a paper towel that is damp but not dripping wet. Roll up the towel and place it in a resealable storage bag. Partially seal the bag and place it in a cool, dry place such as in a drawer or cupboard.

In 2 or 3 days, check to see how many seeds have sprouted. Moldy seeds do not count as sprouted. Discard both the moldy seeds and any seeds that have germinated. Continue to check the seeds daily for up to 2 weeks, if necessary. When you are checking the seeds, moisten the paper towel, if needed.

Discontinue the test early if all seeds have been counted.

Calculate your germination rate. If, at the end of 2 weeks, 4 of 10 seeds have sprouted, you have a 40 percent germination rate (5 seeds is equal to a 50 percent rate; 6 seeds, a 60 percent rate; and so on). Most commercial seed companies aim for a 90 to 95 percent germination rate. If your rate was lower and you still want to use your seeds, add extra seeds to each hole to account for the germination rate suggested by your test.

Temperature

If you can find a way to add a week or two to the beginning or last part of the season, you will buy time to invest in extra crops. For instance, plant kale, turnips or leaf lettuce as early as possible and then add another harvest of tomatoes right at the end tail of your season.

When you start to plant earlier than usual when the weather is still cold, make sure you keep the air all around the plants warm. For this, you can use row covers, cold frames, cloches or mulches.

If you want to start your gardening season with vegetables that actually prefer warmer weather conditions, like peppers, melons and eggplants, there is a way. Provide them with an extra blanket of heating the soil as well as the air around them. Start to preheat the cold soil six to eight weeks prior to the last frost. Cover it with IRT, infrared-transmitting mulch or sheets of black plastic. Plastic will absorb the heat from the sun and warm up the soil underneath.

With either of these options in place, cover the whole bed with a tunnel made of clear plastic with slits in it to allow some of the heat to escape if necessary. As soon as the temperature of the soil reaches sixty five to seventy degrees Fahrenheit, you can set out your plants. Now cover the mulch or black plastic using a straw to make sure it does not trap excessive heat. As soon as the danger of more frost is past, or the temperature has risen enough, get rid of the plastic tunnel. Re-install it at the end of summer when the cold set in again.

Harvesting

Harvest time is usually busy, especially if you have planted enough food to preserve, can, dehydrate, or otherwise keep for future use. If you have planted just enough food to eat fresh, harvest season will be more manageable. But, keep in mind, once a garden starts producing, it keeps on producing. What a great time of year!

Harvesting is another task not to put off. Once a veggie is ready to be picked, harvest it and enjoy it. If you leave vegetables on the plant to rot, they will encourage disease and also slow the production of the plant they are on.

Open up your garden journal. You noted when you planted your seeds and seedlings, and you estimated the number of days to harvest, which should help you determine when harvesting will start.

During this season, check your garden daily for any issues and ready-to-pick produce. You don't want to miss out on the bounty of your effort, and as you learned, leaving crops on the plant is an invitation for bugs and disease.

The best time to harvest is morning, when it is not too warm for you or the plants. But I must confess, I walk through the garden at lunch and dinnertime to harvest a couple of items to eat. Nothing beats freshly picked produce that you grew.

Tips on paths for Your Raised Bed Garden

If you are to have multiple raised bed gardens, then you should consider having paths in between the gardens for easy movement. The paths are like the backbone of any garden and they add a sense of beauty and colour to the whole aesthetic outlook. Functional paths will help you reach the key elements of your garden faster.

You should take in a lot of consideration while choosing the final material in which the garden path will be constructed with. Most brick raised beds mostly go with rustic woodchips path around it.

Creating paths using bricks or paving slabs

Paths that are been made with bricks or paving slabs are usually the sturdiest and they allow me to push my wheelbarrow around. You can dig them deep into the soil so that they become one with the ground. Put in some sand or some cement to fill in any leftover holes that may have been left unfiled. Then sprinkle in some water for it to become set.

You can find people who want to sell off their second hand bricks so that you get them at cheaper rates and you don't have to waste your money on brand new bricks.

Making use of grass

This one is a very cheap option, although I do not recommend it fully because of the amount of maintenance that has to be put into it to make it remain neat and fresh. The grasses have to be mowed at least once a week during the growing sessions. I use a shade-tolerant breed of grass to lay my paths so that they remain green all year long.

I have found out that for the path to stay as comfortable as ever, one has to make it as large as 20 inches wide. Remember that you will be pushing your wheelbarrow through those spaces and the space will have to be large enough to be able to contain the equipment for easier movements. A path in which a wheelchair will be used should be as wide as 25 inches so that it will be easy to move through it.

Using gravel to lay the paths

I have come across some paths laid with gravels. Gravel paths are relatively cheap and very easy to construct. The only demerit of using gravel is that once you mistakenly drop soil or compost on it while working, it is quite hard to pack it up and discard.

Most gravel paths I have come across mostly make use of treated lumbers at the boundaries of the path to prevent the gravels from spilling to other sides. Use a roller or a wacker to compact down the ground and make it hold still.

To construct a herringbone brick path

Herringbone brick paths add a lot of overall beauty to the gardens. They give off this rustic effect when they are constructed between beds. I advise most people to go ahead with the method, because they are quite easy to pull through during constructions. Here is a simple step by step procedure that works out fine. To construct a herringbone brick path, you would need some sand and bricks.

- Dig out the soil where the path will be laid out. This is to ensure that the path is flush with the surface. Dig down as deep as 1 inch more than the height of the bricks that will be used.

- Fill in the path with sand up to a thickness of 1 inch.

- Then lay up the bricks in a herringbone pattern along the length of the path.

- Use a hammer to bed the bricks into the ground and brush in more sand into the gaps to fill up the gaps.

What Is Raised Bed Gardening

There is not one solid definition for the term. Different sizes, shapes, and designs that look entirely unique from each other can all fall into the category of raised bed. Rather, the term should be considered as a category under which many different approaches to gardening fit. Think of it almost like a movie genre. You have action movies but then under action movies are car flicks and martial arts films. They're all different but they share the same overall qualities.

We can extrapolate some information from the term itself. The fact that we are speaking about a raised bed means that we are planting our seeds above the ground level. How far above the ground level is up to the individual gardener. Your raised bed may only be raised up a couple feet off the ground but this isn't always the case. If you have ever seen a bed of flowers attached to a windowsill then you've seen another kind of raised bed. Windowsill beds tend to be at waist level (at the lowest) or chest level (at the higher end of the spectrum). So while the height varies quite a bit, the one definite thing that we can agree on is that the bed itself is above ground.

Another feature that is common among the various kinds of raised beds is the inclusion of a frame. Regardless of what the frame is made out of, its purpose is to separate the growing environment inside the bed from the natural environment around it. This frame is packed with nutritious soil and the walls of the frame prevents it from spilling out. Many gardeners choose locations that will allow them access to all four sides of their bed, however this isn't a feature of the raised bed itself but rather a product that arises from the gardener's design choices. Raised beds alongside windowsills don't offer this ability but that doesn't prevent them from being raised beds, after all.

While a frame is typical, they don't necessarily need to have a bottom. Many include a bottom to further separate the growing environment from the natural world but this feature isn't a given. However, a bottom will help to prevent pests from getting into your garden and we'll be treating the raised beds in this book as if they have a bottom.

So the prime characteristics that we use to identify and discuss raised bed gardens throughout the remainder of the book can be broken down into three features. These are beds that are above ground level, even if only one or two feet. They are designed to create a unique growing space which the gardener has total control of and which is separated from the natural world around it. Finally, these raised beds use a frame along the sides and the bottom in order to keep everything in place. When these three features are present, you have yourself a raised bed garden.

Different Materials to Build Your Raised Bed

Wood or Scaffolding Boards.

The lumber we can purchase now will generally be treated with ACQ and another compound CA-B (Copper Azole) they both have a fungicide and copper but not any arsenic. The purpose of the copper compound is to deter pests and insects and the fungicide in the compound is there to restrict the soil fungi migrating into the wood. The fungicide in AQC is quat, which is used in swimming pool chemicals and disinfectants. CA-B is a fungicide, which is used on food crops and is made up of copper and tebuconazole. In short, copper-infused lumber to use as a project such as a raised garden bed is considered safe to grow food crops.

If you have existing wood in your garden that you are thinking of using for your raised bed it's worth considering testing the wood to see if it has been treated with CCA. The continued migration of the arsenic into your plot, even if you are not using the wood in your raised bed will affect the whole area eventually, migrating into your rich soil for your crops.

Pinewood is another alternative and the attraction is the cost which is much lower than say redwood or cedar however it will not last as long as such hardy woods. But it's easy to source and easy to manage too. The wood you select will, of course, differ greatly from region to region, but the best choice and quite often the most cost-efficient, is locally sourced, with an FSC (Forest Stewardship Council) certification. It doesn't have the great aesthetic that hardwoods give and you will have to pay more for organically treated pine. Personally, I wouldn't use treated pine unless it was safe to grow my crops and my thoughts are if you do, it will be at the back of your mind that your produce may be contaminated due to high percentage of chemicals used, I believe it's better to start as you mean to carry on.

Cedar, redwood, Juniper, and Yew are all naturally rot-resistant and extremely durable and long lasting and do give a great look and finish to your garden if your budget allows. There is a reason many choose these types of wood and find them superior, their durability and versatility as well as their aesthetic and the fact they are easy to work with. The downside is the cost is usually twice the price of say pine; also they are not very sustainable as hardwoods are slower growers.

When visiting your lumber yard it's a great practice to note what sizes the lumber comes in, that way you can tailor your raised bed to this exact size minimising any waste cuts. 8-foot lengths by 4-foot widths are a perfect size for me, but this may not work for you.

Wooden Frame Kits

Some will be reading this thinking about how lazy can you be, but some people just don't have the time and ability to source materials to self-build, you can find these at a lot of hardware or garden stores and of course Amazon. They are pre-made garden bed kits that come in a variety of sizes, are well priced and easy to construct. The downsides are some of the quality, certainly of the wood isn't always the greatest (you don't always know the country of origin either) so it may not be durable and long lasting. Also once constructed and filled you may find because of poor durability and strength you may see some bowing under the strain of the moist earth. Certainly, if it's starting to bow at that point, rest assured on the first heavy downpour it will worsen. Not all are built this way though so if this is the option you want, have a good hunt around and look at reviews, etc. to make sure it is right for your project.

Brick Built Raised Beds

These can be time-consuming and require some skill to build; however, they are built to last and will serve you well for years to come plus if built well they look stunning in your garden. You will need a string, a spirit level (use it at every given opportunity to get perfectly level walls!) bricks, and a hard-core base of rubble. Don't forget to leave regular gaps between brick joints to allow room for drainage; you can go ahead at the end to cover these holes with mesh to stop any clogging.

Another alternative to brick is to use blocks or concrete panels which will require rendering to give a polished finish, these methods do offer good insulation for your plants at a reasonably low cost too. The downside though is if you needed to move your bed it would be troublesome to relocate. Also, you may find over time it could crack or sink.

Railway Sleeper Raised Beds

A very popular choice is to use old rustic looking railway sleepers which give a great aesthetic to any garden, however most authentic or vintage ones will have been treated with tar and creosote which will inevitably be transferred into your nutrient-rich soil and affect the quality of your crops.

They can be pricey to purchase, although if you hunt around you can find a good deal at salvage yards, also not all are the same size so some adaptation will be required to get the sizing right for your raised bed.

If this is the look you want for your raised bed I would seriously consider softwood sleepers that have been treated with eco-friendly preservatives. The bonus is no nasty chemicals to tarnish your crops and also lighter material to handle while constructing, a bit more pricey but overall the better option of the two.

Now you have decided on what you are building with and sourced the materials you now need to prepare the area before you actually build the bed.

When preparing the land you need to ensure that the area is reasonably level, don't worry too much if you are thinking of shallow root system crops but for deeper root system crops (carrots, parsnips, etc.) it would be worth breaking the soil surface on the area and digging to appropriately 30cm depth, removing any rocks and debris that would hinder healthy root growth. But if you are building your bed no deeper than 14-16 inches high, then I recommend lifting the grass and sod from the surface and inverting it before construction.

Using string and stakes mark out the dimensions of your raised bed. Using a spirit level at all times will ensure you get a straight, even raised bed. If you have ordered the exact size for your raised bed from the hardware store, go ahead and begin to use the screws to attach the timber lengths together. If not, cut to size and attach. Don't forget to measure twice and cut once!

Screws will last longer and are easier if you want to move the raised bed at any time, however, nails are easier to work with and quicker. If you find you have difficulty getting the screws in you can pre-drill the holes. Always use galvanized fixtures to protect from corrosion if your budget allows.

If you are concerned with small rodents being able to get into your construction, you can opt to line the bed with a metal hardware cloth or mesh (1/4 or 1/2") to the bottom of the bed. Using staples to attach is the easiest method.

Avoiding the use of plastic if possible as the toxins can leach into the soil and contaminate your plants; it will also contribute to discouraging the much-needed earthworms and insects and have a detrimental effect on your drainage. The assembly of the raised bed if you are using timber, is best done on-site. Using posts on all corners will help with the overall structure and sturdiness. This will ensure once your raised bed is filled with earth, it will stop the walls from bowing or even collapsing depending on the height and volume.

Internal corner posts 2" x 2" timber should be added to give stability, depending on the height of your raised bed but roughly 15-18" deep. If you do decide on a larger raised bed add additional wooden stakes in at every 5 feet for ultimate support against the volume of soil.

Move the assembled bed into place. Check to make sure that everything is level if you find it is not (It may not be!) put the box aside and use a shovel to level the ground. You can use builders' sand to level the area if it is uneven in places. Put the box back and check again using a mallet to tap down the boards and make an indent. Take a look at your marked plan on the plot and mark out where your corners of the box are. This will give you indicators where you will dig down for your four corner posts. This is the perfect time to check once again you have adequate space to comfortably move around the raised bed you have just marked. You want to be able to get to your plants from all angles, so if you find you have miss-calculated your plan, this is the time to reassess and adjust to ensure you have free movement right around the perimeter of your raised bed.

Once you have checked the location is perfect, moving the box away again, dig in 1-foot deep holes at each of your marked corners. It's best practice to use a speed square to mark the timber at all four sides of the corner posts once cut at roughly 1 -foot from the end, to indicate how deep your posts will go into the ground. These marks are your guide to where you will line up and attach your constructed box to the posts. Now you can attach the box to the four corner posts. Next set the box, with attached corner posts onto the marked ground. Resting the four corner posts into the pre-dug holes. Check the construct with a spirit level and ensure everything is perfectly level.

Lastly, you can opt to attach decorative finials or capping to the top of each corner post to give a finishing touch and it may also help when watering by stopping the hosepipe running across your raised bed, snapping or breaking your new plants.

Another great feature that you can use, which is under-utilized, and is fantastic for people in colder climates, is converting their raised beds into a poly-tunnel. To do this add three pieces of plastic plumbing pipe evenly spaced along each long side, in which you can insert a smaller diameter flexible plastic pipe. This will go up and over your garden bed and inserting it into the plastic on the opposite side of the bed creating a hoop. Then you can stretch plastic over them to create a dome. This will save space and time and money. Also, it will generously increase your overall yield.

What To Plant

If you haven't yet figured out what you want to grow in your raised bed garden then this chapter is for you. There are a lot of options available to you, though the primary factor limiting them is your local climate. You won't be able to grow plants that need tons of sun if you don't have much and instead live in a colder area. However, once you move past this obstacle then you will find that there are plenty of plants that do great in a raised bed.

A raised garden bed is pretty much exactly the same as a regular garden bed but with some added benefits such as better drainage. If you could grow a plant in the ground in your local area then you can grow it in a raised bed garden. However, there are some plants that do better in a raised bed than the ground. One example is succulents. These plants come from hot and dry areas and they like to have a soil that is very sandy, even to the point of being rocky. While too much moisture will rot just about any plant's roots, succulents are especially prone to it. The added draining speed that comes from raising up a garden bed for succulents will help them to survive and thrive much easier than if they were just in the ground. In fact, if you are going to grow succulents at all then I absolutely suggest either a raised bed or an elevated position in the ground if possible.

But succulents are just one (beautiful) example of what you can grow in a raised garden bed. This chapter is filled with tons of others ranging from flowers to veggies and everything in between.

Planting Out Your Raised Bed

When deciding what to plant in your raised bed, there are a number of things to take into consideration. These could include the following:

- How many raised beds do you have to plant? More than one bed means that you can have a larger crop of one single vegetable kind.

- How big is your family, or how many do you intend to feed?

- Does your raised bed get full sun, i.e. at least 6-8 hours per day?

- What do you like to eat? This may sound like a silly question; however it is easy to grow something just because you can. Only to find that it is wasted at the end of the season because you do not really like Brussel sprouts for instance!

- Did you use this bed last year, and if you did, what did you grow on it? Good crop rotation is key to getting a great harvest.

As you may understand, what to plant is a question that has many answers depending on your individual wants and needs – as well as the wants and needs of your friends and neighbors!

For this reason I will cover a few different planting regimes that hopefully may give you some ideas of your own.

Crop types

First of all we must divide the crops into their respective families, in order to get the best out of the soil conditions they are planted in.

Root Crops: Potatoes, carrots, parsnips, beetroot, fennel, celery

Brassicas: Cabbage, Brussel sprouts, cauliflower, broccoli, radish, swede turnip

Legumes: Peas, mange tout, French and broad beans

Alliums (onion family): Shallots, onions, garlic, chives, leeks

Solanaceae: Aubergine, potato, tomato, peppers, eggplant

Cucurbits: Cucumber, squash, pumpkin, melon, marrow

Miscellaneous: All fruits, lettuce, herbs, sweetcorn, chicory, asparagus

Though this is by no means an extensive list, it does give a good selection of the most commonly grown vegetables, and is more than enough to get started with!

Watch your height

One of the things that is easy to over-look, but most important, is to be aware of the height of the plants. Plant the high plants or climbers in the north end of the bed, that way they will not shade the rest of your crop from the all-important–life-giving–sunlight.

In other words, if you have a raised bed that is broadside on to the sun for most of the day, then perhaps a frame built along the back of the bed would be a good idea. This would enable you to grow runner beans, peas or cucumber plants, making an excellent backdrop to the vegetables in the rest of the bed.

Peas would have the added advantage of adding nitrogen to the soil that would ensure a great harvest from the likes of cabbage or cauliflower that are particularly nitrogen hungry plants. It is also true however, that all plants like some nitrogen in their diet of nutrients, and so this technique would benefit just about everything.

A single crop

Planting a single crop in a raised bed is usually only done if you have more than one bed in which to grow your vegetables. After all what is the point in growing just one crop, unless of course you are a fanatical pumpkin grower, or just cannot see past a good cucumber harvest!

Good crop rotation is not only important as to the nutrient value, but also for pest control and issues such as blight and fungal growth.

Companion crops are vegetables that get on well with other vegetables such as onions, carrots and lettuce or spinach onions and brassicas, being that their nutritional needs are similar, but their root systems collect the nutrients at different levels and so are not truly in direct competition with each other.

As well as giving you a variety of vegetables, this is a good idea for things such as pest control and less weeding as the veg blocks out the light to the weeds; and different crops attract different insects thereby helping control the spread of the insects themselves.

Antagonist crops are crops that do not do so well together such as Alliums (onions and garlic) with peas and bean crops. Crops such as beetroot get along with most plants and so can be planted quite successfully between onions or leeks without any problem.

Mixed crop examples

If you have just one raised bed and are trying out several varieties of vegetables to give you a good mixed crop, then some planting tips could include the following regime:

Tall plants to the back, on a fixed support of some kind where needed.

This could be planted with tomatoes, or peas, runner beans or cucumbers if the climate allows.

Sweet corn could also be used here and companioned with lettuce that will take advantage of the shade from the corn. To the front of the raised bed could go any low-lying crop such as carrot, beetroot, parsnips, etc.

If peppers are your main crop then you could grow spinach between the pepper plants. Again similar to the lettuce and corn example, the spinach will take advantage and flourish in the shade provided by the peppers.

If you stay in a cooler climate such as the UK, then you could try covering a portion of your raised bed with a frame similar to that pictured earlier, and cover with polythene. This will enable you to grow tomatoes and cucumber plants for instance, maybe even some sweet peppers – so expensive to buy in the supermarket!

To get the most out of a mixed crop the idea is about looking at the different vegetables needs regarding hours of sunlight and nutrient requirements. A good idea is to plant vegetables together that have different root systems, as mentioned earlier.

Planting deep rooted vegetables such as carrots or parsnips, means that you can companion them with shallow rooted vegetables such as beetroot, lettuce and arugula (rocket) to make for a good health selection.

Ultimate mixed crop

We can hardly discuss the idea of a mixed crop, without including a piece on the square foot example of growing mixed vegetables.

As mentioned, this is a system that is intensive farming gone to the extreme – but in a good way! The idea is that the old method of growing vegetables in a garden plot, where everything is planted in rows, is made redundant.

Instead we have a situation where a plot of ground – raised or otherwise – is set out in squares 1 foot square. Within these mini-plots a range of vegetables are planted, according to your needs and other deciding factors such as weather, nutrients etc.

The 'sales pitch' if you like, for this style of gardening include the following points:

A large percentage of a traditional vegetable plot is wasted owing to the fact that you must have pathways between the vegetables for weeding, harvesting, etc.

With a proper rotational method of planting, you need never use fertilizer again, as the crops will feed themselves.

Far less waste than a traditional garden where all the cabbages, or cauliflower or whatever, is ready at more or less the same time, and has to be frozen, canned or given away.

Similar to a raised bed, the square foot method does not need such intensive care, due to the close proximity of the plants and the ease of gardening methods, particularly if it is used with conjunction with a raised bed garden.

One of the main strengths of this gardening method is the fact that it uses up very little space, especially if you go for the four foot square method. This means that despite this small space you can grow a complete range vegetables and have them all maturing at different times, depending of course on the length of the growing season. That said, you have to keep a keen eye on any disease or insect infestation, potentially caused by the close proximity and there-fore poor air circulation, in this type of growing environment. A square foot garden design lends itself very well to cultivating a full spectrum of herbs available. This in turn will ensure a garnish for every meal you prepare as well as some great tomato and basil salads for example.

Tips for growing healthy plants

As it has been stated before, plants that are healthy are less susceptible to diseases and pests than those that are less healthy. I try to keep my plants as healthy as possible to help them be able to fight diseases better. Keeping your plants healthy will help to boost their immune system. Here are a few tips that can be employed to ensure that your plants stay healthy and are able to protect themselves from diseases.

1. Ensure that they are well fed and watered.

2. Build and environment in the garden that will conducive enough for beneficial insects and predators. This can encourage wildlife that will help dispel smaller pests. For example ladybugs and lacewings feed on aphids and birds and hedgehogs feed on slugs.

3. You can employ biological controls such as nematodes which can be used to combat snails on hostas or vine weevil in containers.

4. Select plant species that more resistant to certain diseases e.g. some carrot species are more resistant to carrot fly than others.

5. I am in the league of those farmers who believe that growing some plants close to others can have mutual benefits for both of the plants. This is popularly known as companion planting. For example, carrot and onion being planted together can provide both of the plants with some benefits. Onion fly are deterred by the smell of carrots and so is carrot fly deterred by the smell of onion.

6. Grow your plants spaciously so that air will be able to circulate effectively around the raised bed. I make use of a small rake to clear away any fallen leaves or rotting fruits from the floor. You should be vigilant and remove any infected material from the plant as soon as you can spot it.

a. Where will I site my raised bed garden?

Plants and vegetables are never going to survive for long without sunlight. It is an essential part of their diet. The more the sunshine, the higher the tendency for your garden to flourish. On average, plants need about eight hours of sunlight daily. So, this means your choice of location is highly dependent on where in your yard receives the most amount of sunlight.

Another thing to consider in locating your raised bed gardens is the type of soil you have present within your yard. As much as you can import a whole lot of compost soil from outside, it is crucial to see if the ground within your space is usable for such an exercise. This test will help cut down costs and will ease incorporation. So, in an event where you find out that your yard indeed has a significant amount of soil that will adequately support plant life, it would be a shame if you don't use them. Please ensure that before you use the soil from your yard for planting within the frames, and that it is entirely rid of weeds, grasses, and debris that won't impede plant growth.

If your number of besteads is much, then buying soil in large amounts will suffice. They come in a cubic foot, cubic yard or cubic meter. When making your purchase, you can demand about sixty percent topsoil, thirty percent compost and about ten percent potting soil, which contains essential plant nutrients contained in perlite, vermiculite and peat moss.

There are other options to explore in the case where finding quality soil is hard to come by. A mixture of compost and potting soil at equal proportions will serve wonderfully.

b.What type of raised gardens will I adopt?

What do I plant?

Your choice of what to plant will significantly influence other critical decisions about your chosen adventure.

First, make up your mind on whether you would be planting for aesthetics or consumption. Planting for aesthetics will require that you consider the type of materials to use, how high above the ground and the variety of shapes to employ. Planting for consumption, on the other hand, will require particular focus on soil type, depth, and sizes of bedsteads.

In both cases, you are encouraged to choose out of a pool of your favorite plants. Plant to what you love to eat- tomatoes, peppers, potatoes, cucumbers, etc. you can choose to have a mixture of consumption and beautiful plants. Just ensure that you don't plant them tightly together as this will increase competition for nutrients and air circulation.

It's vital that you research on the growing habits of the plants you choose. Some are crawlers, and others are climbers. Some are root plants, while others are tubers. Read up on your preferred choices. Also, it's essential that you read up on which plants would be right to grow together. While planting tomatoes with cabbages is fine, planting tomatoes with crawling cucumbers can prove to be challenging.

Finally, do your research on how to effectively grow your plant, taking into cognizance the prevailing climate within your region. Some plants may not need to be planted from seed level in your garden because the favorable weather which they may require might be gone long before they reach harvest. So, it would be best to purchase them from a nursery and transplant. In any case, the onus is on you to do thorough research before making your choices and proceeding to plant.

When do I plant?

This question is an important one. Your answer will be determined your choice of plants, the current climate within your region and at what level you choose to do your planting.

Some plants thrive in cold weathers; broccoli, for example; but tomatoes will die out in such cold temperatures. With each plant, there are best times to plant them. You must do your research and put down frost dates and take note of soil temperatures. Under no condition should you grow any plant that is averse to cold when the frost hasn't passed.

As some plants are opposed to low temperatures, so are others that can't survive in extreme temperatures. Be careful to figure out what your garden choices may require. On average, most plants do well in reasonable soil temperatures of between sixty to seventy degrees Fahrenheit.

In the event where you embark on transplanting, it is vital that you do so when temperatures are average, and the weather is just right. In the case where you transplant and the weather turns out to be harsh, then you'll have to cover them up for the meantime and shield them from intense sunlight and dry winds.

Herbs You Can Grow At Home

Anise

Salads, cookies, cheese, and candies are the most common foods that utilize this herb. Aside from being used as a fragrance in creams and soaps, it is also a common ingredient in expectorants and medicines for upset stomach. Anise is easy to grow but requires full sun exposure as well as well-drained soil.

How to Grow Anise Seed

1. Seeds directly sown into a container is the only way to grow anise. Its pot should have holes at the bottom to ensure proper drainage.

2. Cover the seed with lightweight alkaline soil. The seed should be one-fourth or half inch below the soil. Make sure that the soil has 6.3 to 7.0 pH levels and it is mixed with sterile potting mix.

3. Space the seedlings or thin plants up to 18 inches apart in rows one foot apart. The soil should be free from debris, roots, and weeds.

4. You'll need to water them during the dry season at least once or twice every week. You may use a spray bottle to avoid disturbing seeds that are shallowly planted.

5. The soil's temperature should be around 60 to 72 degrees Fahrenheit to achieve best germination. You may maintain the soil's temperature by covering the pot with plastic wrap and then with newspaper sheets.

6. The germination period normally takes two weeks, and during these times, you should always ensure that the soil is moist. After the germination period, remove the plastic wrap and expose the plant to sunlight.

7. You can supplement the plant with a general-purpose fertilizer once or even twice during its growing season. You can also use nitrogen fertilizer to nourish the plant before it starts to flower, especially during June or July.

It can take around four months within a warm growing season to raise the plant. The best time to harvest is anytime within August or September once the flowers transform into seeds or fruits.

Basil

There are plenty of dishes you can incorporate basil too, especially Italian, Thai, and Mediterranean cuisines. For this herb to grow, it needs bright light and warm temperatures. It grows best in well-drained soil.

How to Grow Basil

1. First, you need to decide which basil variety you want to grow. There are many kinds, such as cinnamon basil, lemon basil, purple basil, and Thai basil. You can plant annual basils or perennial basils that grow year after year.

2. In planting basil, you'll need to sow seeds near a sunny window or in a greenhouse, in early spring or a month before the last frost. Then you can transplant them during the early summer season.

3. Make sure that the soil is free from air pockets and then plant one or two seeds in every container. You also need to cover the plants with kitchen wraps until they grow or emerge.

4. Water the plants twice every day and transplant them to permanent containers once the leaves sprout. Make sure that they get sufficient sunlight exposure in the location where you transplant them.

5. Once already established, regular pruning allows the plant to grow to its maximum potential. Get rid of the plant's flower buds once they appear and avoid using any fertilizer as this can reduce the fragrance and flavor of the herb.

If the stems look thin and tall, it means that the plants are not receiving a sufficient amount of sunlight they need. Always ensure that the soil is moist by watering it twice daily. You can choose to plant lemon basil as it is a fast-growing variety and is more productive.

Borage

This herb is well-known for medicinal purposes as it helps reduce fever, fight depression, relieve diarrhea, and treat bronchitis. Borage is popular for its star shape, bright blue flowers, and decorative uses in the culinary world.

How to Grow Borage

1. You can grow borage from seeds planted during early spring if you want it to flower during summer. Sow the seed during autumn if you want spring flowering.

2. Transplantation is not an option once this herb sprouts, so make sure to plant seeds directly into its container. The soil should also be moist and mulched. It is also best that you choose a sandy soil type in planting borage.

3. Select a sunny spot and remember not to cover the seeds completely, as they need direct sunlight to sprout. However, you can also plant it in the partially shaded part of the patio.

4. Establish the right positioning by leaving 2 feet of space between the plants. Borage can spread and take space, so you need to position them a bit apart from each other.

5. Do not forget to water regularly and make sure that you do not end up overwatering the plants. You should fertilize it once per month, especially during the growing season.

When flowers start to appear typically within six weeks after sowing the seeds, you may start the harvest. You can use the flowers and leaves for cake decorations, garnish in salads, or the sprigs in fruit drinks.

Chamomile

Chamomile has always been used for tea but is also a good ingredient for tonics to treat stomach aches. You can choose from Roman chamomile or German chamomile. These have different growing needs. The former is perennial that can grow to about 1 foot while the latter is annual that can reach up to three feet tall.

How to Grow Chamomile

1. You can initially grow the plant indoors in late winter or a month to 6 weeks prior to the last frost. Make sure that there are two to three seeds in each hole before covering with a potting mixture.

2. Cover the plant with a plastic wrap and place it just near the window. It will give the plant sunlight exposure that is moderate and not too intense.

3. Check the plant every day and make sure that the soil is not dry to avoid the "damping off" disease that can potentially kill the seeds.

4. When it starts to germinate, detach the plastic and transfer the container to a sunny window. It will give the plant the amount of heat and sunlight that it needs to survive. When transplanting the herbs, make sure that you leave eight to ten inches of space between the plants.

5. When watering them, use a hose that has a spray nozzle to avoid disturbing the seedlings. Water regularly until the plant is continually growing.

Chamomiles typically grow flowers after one month and when you start harvesting, make sure that you do it carefully. Harvest the blossoms without harming the stems and dry them in a well-ventilated area.

Chives

This perennial herb comes from the family of onions, commonly used in soup, egg, and vegetable dishes. Chives are herbs that you can grow at home since they do not require too much sunlight but are very prolific. It grows well in drained soil, although it can still tolerate low quality or poor soil.

How to Plant Chives

1. When planting chives, you'll need to sow seeds during spring or fall, preferably within ten weeks prior to the last spring frost.

2. Plant the herb two to four inches deep and twelve to eighteen inches apart in moist and healthy soil. You can mix the soil with compost before planting the herb.

3. Make sure that the plant gets full sunlight exposure. You should also get rid of weeds and ensure that the plant is free from diseases.

4. Once the seedlings have established their root system, you can set the rows six inches apart. In maintaining chives, just water them daily and provide necessary sunlight exposure.

5. Avoid excessive use of nitrogen fertilizers. You also need to make sure that the soil has a temperature of 60 degrees to 70 degrees Fahrenheit.

When chives start blooming, you can pinch off the flowers and flower stems to ensure a larger crop. You can start cutting chives when they have already grown two inches above the soil.

Cilantro

This Mexican herb is fast growing and usually adds taste to salads, salsa, and seafood dishes. Cooks around the globe use different parts of cilantro. You can choose to grow this herb in a container or directly in the garden.

How to Plant Cilantro

1. Plan the right location to grow the herb. Cilantros can grow up to 3 feet tall, and this is something that you should consider before starting to plant them.

2. You can start propagation through seeds. You can plant them an inch below the soil and 12 inches apart from each other.

3. Keep the soil below 75 degrees Fahrenheit to keep the roots cool. You can do this by sheltering the herb from direct sunlight exposure or planting it during early spring. You may position the herb near a tree where it gets filtered sunlight.

4. You'll need to keep the soil moist but not too soaked regularly. It requires good drainage since it has deep roots. The soil should also be airy, light, and fast draining with lots of perlites and sharp sand.

5. Use mulch to get rid of weeds, retain moisture, and keep the roots cool. Always remember that when the soil does not drain well, it attracts diseases.

6. Water the plant once or twice a week. It is also wise to cut down the flower heads to let the plant focus on producing greens. You can also take care of your plant more by using nitrogen fertilizer as it can significantly help the leaves develop.

Since it is a short-lived plant, you'll need to sow seeds every few weeks to have a fresh supply of young plants. You can start harvesting once the stalks are already six inches tall. Consume cilantro when fresh because it loses flavor as it dries.

Cumin

Cumin, otherwise called Comino, is an herb usually added to Middle East, Indian, Mediterranean, as well as Mexican cuisines. It is famous for the bold flavor that it provides to starch and meat dishes. It also works effectively in treating indigestion and stomach ailments.

How to Grow Cumin

1. Cumin needs to grow from seeds and benefits from crowding as they help each other to grow. You may start planting indoors eight weeks before the last frost. Cover the seeds with potting soil in a sunny spot of the garden. The soil should be well-drained and has little nitrogen to retain the aroma or fragrance of the seeds.

2. Water the plant regularly and make sure that you do it with care. You can make use of a spray nozzle to keep the seeds from being washed away. Keep the soil and seeds moist until they sprout. It has to be watered frequently, especially during the dry season.

3. Although the spacing does not matter too much, you can transplant the herbs three to four inches away from each other. This herb needs full sun exposure and grows well in either hot weather or damp conditions.

You may harvest the pods once they start opening up and spilling their seeds. Place them in a bag, hang them to dry, and beat the bag to encourage the pods to release the seeds. You can use the herb whole or ground in preparing a variety of delectable dishes.

Dill

Dill is a fragrant and powerfully flavored annual herb that is widely used to improve the taste of soups and sauces. It can grow up to four feet and can attract good insects in your garden.

How to Plant Dill

1. Make sure that you start planting in the later part of spring or during the first days or weeks of summer.

2. Choose a place where you can continually grow the herb since it does not transplant well. The location should be dry, sunny, and protected from strong winds.

3. Sow the seeds a fourth of an inch below a rich and well-drained soil. The soil's temperature should be 60 degrees to 70 degrees Fahrenheit. Bear in mind that the herb can tolerate poor soil as long as it is well-drained.

4. Water the plant well, especially during hot weather and its growing season. Make sure that it is moist and not soaked. Once the plant reaches six to eight inches high, you will need to thin out your plants.

5. If the soil you utilized in growing dill contains plenty of organic matter, then no additional fertilizer is necessary. Provide support and use a bamboo stick for the plant to grow upon. It is especially important if you are residing in a windy climate.

6. Plants should start growing after two weeks. Start harvesting after two months or when the plant has grown four to five leaves. Make sure to cut the area closest to the stem when harvesting.

You can choose a fern leaf dill as it is an ideal addition in cooking salads and fish dishes. You can plant the herb next to vegetables such as onions or cabbage but keep it away from carrots.

Fennel

This multipurpose plant can either be a seasoning through its aromatic seeds or a vegetable through its thick bulb, and like celery, its stalks are also edible. The fennel bulb is an excellent ingredient in many Mediterranean dishes. It is rich in potassium, calcium, fiber, and vitamin C.

How to Grow Fennel

1. Plant fennel directly in its container as it does not transplant well. In planting, you'll need to sow groups of three or four seeds during mid-spring, one-fourth inch deep and eighteen inches apart.

2. Loosen up the soil and mix some compost to add more nutrients. You can also add sand to enhance the container's drainage system. You must grow fennel in fertile, well-drained soil under the full exposure of the sun.

3. Cover the seeds with one-eight inch of soil. Make sure that if you are also growing dills, you keep both plants away from each other as they tend to cross-pollinate. During its growing season, you do not need to fertilize this herb.

4. The herb is easy to grow and only requires you to water it regularly and deeply. You should keep watering the plant until it shows its first leaves. However, avoid over watering it because fennels rot easily.

5. The seeds will germinate in eight to twelve days. Once the bulb starts to develop, protect it from the sun to keep its sweetness and its color. Harvest once the bulb grows into the size of a small tennis ball.

How To Plant

By now you already what to grow and it is time to plant them. Though you still need to make a couple decisions on how you want to do this. First off you will need to decide if you want to plant seeds into your raised garden bed or if you want to start seeds individually to transplant seedlings to the raised bed. If you decide on sowing seeds directly then you have a couple choices on how to do it. We'll cover these first then learn everything there is to know about transplanting seedlings into your outdoor beds.

Guidelines on how to Plant

Starting from seeds, there are a few things to consider. First, remember that you can't plant them into the ground until after the last frost of the winter. Also remember that you shouldn't sow seeds when it is raining out. You can choose whether you want to pay special attention to the sowing step or not but raised garden beds will make the process quicker and easier than it normally is. That said, you should also avoid sowing seeds during windy weather as well since seeds can easily blow away depending on their needs.

How deeply you plant your seeds and how much soil you cover them with afterwards is going to differ between species. Some seeds like to be buried half an inch under the soil but there are others which need the energy from direct sunlight in order to germinate properly. If these were buried under the soil then they would never fully grow into seedlings because they wouldn't have the energy to break out of the shell. In general though, most seeds are going to want to be half an inch to a quarter inch below the surface of the soil. Regardless of depth, almost every type of seed imaginable likes to be watered deeply after it is planted. When planting an entire bed, fully sow the seeds before moving on to watering.

You seed most garden beds one of two ways. On the careful side you drop a couple of seeds into small holes you made in the soil. These are spaced out and weaker plants are trimmed back shortly after sprouting so that each plant has a bit of space around it to grow. The other way that is often used is to take a hoe and dig out a line from one end of the bed to the next. This is repeated as desired, allowing for half a foot to a foot of space between each row depending on the space needs of the intended plant. Seeds are dropped throughout this groove and then the hoe is used to cover it all over. This doesn't offer the same level of control over the placement of the final plants but it keeps everything mostly in a row. If you were doing this directly into the soil then you would also be mixing up and spreading weed seeds while doing this. But in a raised garden bed you don't have this problem. In fact, a raised garden bed offers a third way of sowing seeds that is beginner friendly, though it can be a bit messy.

Since a raised garden bed is filled up with soil that you put there, you know that there aren't any weeds in it and so there is no problem with mixing it up even further. Everything is contained within the bed, so you can throw handfuls of seeds around as you like and then take a hoe and just run through the bed a couple times to make sure everything is mixed up and buried. With no hassle at all, you can sow an entire bed this way. Of course, this is best used when the raised bed is going to be one kind of plant. If you are mixing and matching species in the bed then this will only lead to more mix-ups and weird placements.

That's pretty much all there is to sowing seeds directly into the raised garden bed. Though you will need to thin out the seedlings as they come up, regardless of which method you take. In fact, even when you start seeds indoors you will still find yourself in a situation in which you need to remove some seedlings. Some species, like lettuce, can be eaten when they are still a seedling but most of the time we're simply removing plants that are no longer useful to us. It might seem weird at first but there is only so much room in a single bed and we want to make sure our plants get as many nutrients as they can to stay healthy and produce large harvests and beautiful colors.

Speaking of starting plants indoors, carefully germinating seeds and growing strong seedlings prior to taking the plants outdoors is actually a really great way to get a head start on the season since you can get three-week-old seedlings into the ground the day after the last frost. Of course, it takes more time, effort, and money to start seeds indoors but depending on how you approach gardening, it may be well worth the investment. Seeds shouldn't cost more than a couple of dollars. You will need some soil but we'll just start with a version of our raised bed soil that is a little lighter on the compost. You'll want to get some plastic wrap, perhaps a spray bottle for water. All of that shouldn't cost more than $20. But unfortunately you'll also want to get an LED grow light and this will run $80 on the low end. But LED lights will save you money in the long run because they don't need to be replaced as often and then don't take much electricity. Just make sure the one you purchase is designed for growing vegetables because regular LED lights just won't cut it there. When you have all these pieces, you can start your seeds.

Fill up the small seeding containers with the soil mixture. We use a similar mixture to the soil in our raised garden beds so that transplanting isn't as hard on the plants. However, we use less compost in our mixture because we are working with smaller plants and we don't want to overfeed them. We will give them liquid fertilizer once a week but this will also be at only half or a quarter the strength that we feed our raised garden beds.

Once the containers are all filled, get your seeds ready by planting them each individually. Just use a finger to dig a half inch hole in the soil and drop some seeds. Depending on the size of the plastic trays you are using this could be done only once or twice each container. Drop a few seeds into each hole rather than only one. Some seeds will fail to germinate and so it is always better to have too many seedlings that you need to remove rather than no seedlings at all. Cover or leave the seeds open to the air depending on the type but either way you will want to water the soil entirely. Make sure that water is running throughout the whole of the soil rather than just along the top. Finally, take your plastic wrap and cover up the top of the container then place it under your grow light. How many hours of light they get will depend on what species you are growing.

The plastic wrap is placed over the container to help keep the humidity up. Some plants don't like a lot of humidity but it is pretty much the regular for any vegetables you might be growing. As the seeds are germinating, you are going to want to remove the plastic wrap at least twice a day. One time is to spray water onto the soil with the spray bottle you purchased for exactly that reason. The second time is simply to offer more air to get to the roots of the plant. You might consider using a toothpick to poke holes in the plastic wrap to allow air in. The level of humidity won't stay as high but it might be beneficial to trade a little humidity for oxygen. When spraying with water you only need to soak the top inch. Watering will change after the seedling starts to sprout so pay attention to it. Once it starts to touch the plastic wrap or grow its first set of leaves, whichever happens first, remove the plastic wrap and move onto the next stage. Seeds may take a couple of days or a few weeks to reach this stage depending on the species.

After the plastic wrap is off, you will water your seedlings as is needed. Use a finger to test the top inch of the soil to see if it is dry. When it is, water the seedlings thoroughly. Remember that they aren't very strong yet so water the soil and not the plants themselves. You wouldn't want the water to break a stem or anything. You will need to fertilize them once a week but you should dilute the fertilizer mixture with water so it is only a quarter as strong. Seedlings will typically take two or three weeks to be ready but some take much more. As a rule of thumb, seedlings are ready to be transplanted once they start developing their second set of leaves. However, before you can move an indoor plant into an outdoor raised garden bed, you are going to need to take a week to harden it off.

Hardening off plants is done to prepare indoor plants for a life outside. When they are raised indoors, plants have no reason to develop natural protection from wind and sunlight that they grow when they are started outdoors. You should find a place outside with full shade and protection from the wind. Put the plants outside in this spot for an hour on the first day. Put them out for two hours the second day, three hours the next. Do this over the course of a week, moving the plant into more and more sunlight slowly through the week. This will get the plant used to the outside and it should only take a week for it to start developing natural protections so it can thrive outdoors. After a week of hardening off, it will be time to transplant your seedlings into the raised bed garden.

When seedlings are ready to transplant, make sure you don't move them into the garden until after any wind or rain has stopped and the raised garden bed has a chance to dry out a little. It is best to transplant seedlings early in the morning. Since we have to thoroughly water seedlings after planting, it is best to transplant them early so that there is plenty of time for the water to evaporate before the evening. You should also stop watering your seedlings prior to planting. In fact, you shouldn't water them during the hardening off period except to provide a spray or two of water if they start to wilt too much. Transplanting seedlings is pretty much a dry soil experience.

Take your seedling container and hold two fingers against the base of the plant. Grip it firmly while you rotate and flip over the plant pot. Do this over a bucket or outside so that you don't have to worry about potting soil getting all over the place. As the soil falls out, you should start to see the roots of the seedling. Try not to damage these or to sit them down on any surface you haven't cleaned yet. It is very important to replace these roots carefully but first we should check them to make sure that the seedling is healthy. Roots that are in good health will be white or light brown and those that are infected and rotting will not only be black but they'll also be covered in a slimy residue. This is a sign of root rot from overwatering your seedlings. If you catch it early then you can remove the infected roots before introducing the plant to your raised garden bed. If it hasn't spread to the foliage yet then this will save your plant's life. Always check the roots when transplanting. It isn't good for a plant's health to be digging it up to check the roots and so you should always take a chance to look them over when they are going to be exposed anyway.

You want to plant your seedlings into the raised garden bed so that they're roughly the same height as they were in their original container. You will want to dig out a little hole in the soil to set the roots into. Carefully cover the roots with soil and pack it in tightly around the base of the plant's stem to keep it firm and not wobbling around. Water the seedling fully and then check on it over the next couple of days. It might look a little weak at first but you should see it start to stand up tall and grow strong. It is a good idea to transplant seedlings about halfway between receiving fertilizer and the following application. This will allow the soil enough time to dry out so that fertilizing and watering can continue as usual.

Starting your seeds indoors may make for a lot more work but the rewards speak for themselves. Bigger plants at the start of the growing season can result in large yields or even an extra harvest but that comes at the cost of a LED grow light and the time it takes to properly germinate seeds and put them through hardening off and transplanting. If you have the time and resources to do it, starting indoors is the way to go but that doesn't mean sowing directly into the ground is necessarily a bad idea. It can have results in the same range for much less effort but it does invite more randomness and chances for error where indoor starting offers gardeners more control over the process. Ultimately, you will have to decide for yourself which is the right way to go when it comes to your raised bed gardens.

Hydroponics Vs Raised Bed Gardening

The Advantages of Hydroponics

There are a number of factors you consider before choosing a new way of doing things. The same applies to hydroponics. From your perspective, as a grower, the main factors you think about are quality of produce, yield, and efficiency. However, these are not the only benefits you stand to enjoy when working with hydroponics. You need to think long-term. Below are some of the benefits of using hydroponics:

- Overcome soil challenges

Hydroponics allows you to grow plants anywhere, whether you have limited access to soil, the soil is toxic, or you don't have access to growth space at all. On the same note, you don't have to worry about most of the challenges you normally experience with growing plants in soil, such as pests and diseases. A lack of access to arable land should not stop you from growing plants anymore.

- Maximize location and space utility

Everything your plants need is available and maintained within the hydroponics system. Because of this, you can grow the plants anywhere, even in your spare bedroom, as long as there is sufficient space to set up. Plant roots do not need to stretch and expand to find oxygen and food. Everything they need is available in the nutrient solution provided. This also means that you can grow your plants close to one another without worrying about space allocation.

- Freedom from climate constraints

One of the benefits of hydroponic growing is that you have full control over the important climate conditions, such as air composition, intensity of light, humidity, and temperature. This allows you the freedom to grow plants throughout the year, no matter the prevailing weather conditions in your area. In case you are a business farmer, you can produce plants at opportune moments during the year to maximize your profit potential.

- Save on water consumption

Another benefit of using hydroponics is that you get to save water in the process. This system uses around 10% of water compared to normal soil growth. Other than that, you recycle and reuse runoff water back into the system. The only way you lose water in this system is through evaporation or if you have a faulty hydroponics system that leaks. Considering that ground agriculture is responsible for most of the surface and groundwater consumption, switching to hydroponics is a brilliant idea.

- Nutritional value

Since you are fully in control of the nutrients that your plants need, there is little room for nutrient wastage. You can research the plants you want to grow and their nutritional needs at each stage in their growth cycle, then use this information to provide sufficient nutritional cover. Since the nutrients are contained within the growth tank, there is no loss through absorption into the soil.

- Controlling the pH

Each crop has a specific pH level at which it thrives. All the minerals you need in hydroponics are in the water. Therefore, you can make adjustments to the pH levels of water based on the mixture you need for each plant. This way, you provide the necessary nutrients without upsetting the pH balance.

- Faster growth

Compared to plants grown in the soil, hydroponics plants grow faster. You control all the growth conditions necessary for your plants. This way, you can provide the ideal condition for plant growth down to the finest detail. Since plants no longer have to struggle for nutrition, the energy that would be spent is channeled toward fruit production and optimum growth.

- Weeds, pests, and diseases

One of the challenges you deal with whenever you are growing plants in the soil is weeding. Weeds can be quite a headache in that they choke your plants, and at the same time, consume a lot of your time. Since weeds predominantly thrive on soil, doing away with soil in hydroponics eliminates the weed problem for you.

Other than weeds, without using soil, your plants are no longer at a high risk for pests and diseases, such as Pythium and Fusarium. You also don't need to worry about an invasion from locusts, birds, or any other pests. By controlling the growth environment, your risk of these deterrents is much lower than someone who is growing through the normal method.

- Limited use of herbicides and insecticides

Your exposure to pests and diseases is drastically reduced in the absence of soil. This also means that your use of chemicals in the growth process is also limited. As a result, you have a higher chance of growing healthier plants. The need for food safety at the moment is at an all-time high, and since hydroponics allows you to cut down on herbicide and insecticide use, it is a good alternative for gardening.

- Time and labor intensity

You save a lot of time and labor through hydroponics in terms of cultivation, watering, tilling, and other tasks necessary. The techniques used in hydroponics will also save you on the cost of repair and maintenance for equipment.

- Aesthetic appeal

The aesthetic appeal of hydroponics growth is another benefit you will appreciate. You can take care of your hydroponics farm easily without worrying about wandering through large fields. You can grow anything from fresh vegetables to herbs, fruits, and flowers and relax in the beauty before you.

The Disadvantages of Hydroponics

While there are many benefits of using hydroponics, it is not always an easy experience. There are challenges you might face in the process that you should be aware of. Preparing adequately for these challenges increases the prospect of success for your venture.

- Considerable investment

Each time you discuss an alternative way of doing things, it is common to assume costs will be affordable. However, this is not always the truth. A hydroponic garden needs a lot of your time, and in some cases, money. In a traditional soil garden, your plants will grow on their own, fend for themselves, and so on. There is little else for you to do concerning their growth. On the other hand, a hydroponic garden needs constant attention and considerable knowledge about what to use, how to use it, and when.

In a hydroponic garden, your plants depend on you for everything. From the initial installation, you must take care of the plants until they mature. If you plan on expanding the growth of your plants to commercial purposes, a simple water culture system might not be sufficient. You have to consider investing in an active system, which means buying pumps and other appliances. You will also need to automate the process. Automation calls for maintenance and considerable checks all around.

- Knowledge and technical experience

There are a lot of types of equipment you will use when running a hydroponic garden, especially for commercial purposes. You must know the growth process for each plant, the requirements and adequate light conditions, how far it should be away from the light bulb, and so on. Without this technical knowledge, you might struggle to raise a successful hydroponic garden. It gets more challenging when you are growing more than one plant species. You must know the fine details about each plant and factor it into the nutrient solution.

- Electricity and water challenges

Two of the most important elements in your hydroponic garden are water and electricity. A hydroponic garden does consume less water than a typical soil garden. However, you are constantly running a system in which water and electricity are in close proximity, and this creates a huge risk. You must have adequate safety measures in place, particularly if you are running a commercial operation. Other than that, you need a backup plan in place in case of blackouts. If your plants go without water for a long time, the roots will dry out.

- Initial cost

Depending on the expected size of your garden, your initial setup cost might run into a few hundreds of dollars or even higher. Some of the equipment you need include growth media, nutrients for each plant, a timer, pump, and lights. However, once your setup is complete, the only things you will have to spend on are electricity bills for lighting and running the water system and the cost of nutrients.

- Spreading diseases

One of the benefits of hydroponic gardens is that you don't have to deal with the conventional challenges involved in growing a typical soil garden, especially pests and diseases. However, there is always a risk that any disease that affects your plants could escalate to other plants within the same nutrient reservoir. However, this should not be a big problem for you, considering that the likelihood of diseases affecting plants in a hydroponic garden is so low.

Advantages of Raised Bed Gardening

There are several advantages that a raised bed has over planting straight into the ground, some of these are as follows:

With a raised bed, it really does not matter what quality your garden soil is, or indeed what the drainage is like. As this is all added when forming your raised bed garden.

Easy to service/maintain. With a raised bed you have the advantage of height, which means that you do not have to bend over as far to take care of your vegetables. This is particularly advantageous if you are prone to suffer from backache.

Weed free. A raised bed is not troubled to nearly the same extent by the incursion of weeds, as all the soil/compost mix is freshly added. For any weeds that do appear, they are easier to remove as the compost mix does not compact like garden soil.

It is far easier to control destructive pests within a raised bed garden. This is simply because you are off the ground, and so keeping a natural barrier up in front of creeping pests like garden slugs. With a slightly higher raised bed of around two feet, then you are not troubled quite as much with carrot fly for instance, who tend to be low fliers.

So out with back-breaking weeding tasks, along with digging over water logged soil and filtering out rocks and stones. In with easy gardening methods for the busy householder, and fresh vegetables for the whole family with the minimal of hassle.

The Disadvantages of a Raised Bed Garden

Raised bed gardening is one of those things where the positives far outweigh the negatives. But, the reality is, there are negatives surrounding the method as well. For instance—

- Raised bed gardening requires a certain degree of construction before you can get started. You need to construct the walls of the bed itself or purchase one at a local gardening store.

- To ensure the quality of soil, especially if your garden isn't ideal for planting, you may need to purchase good soil as well.

- While it minimizes efforts for soil maintenance, the idea that it doesn't require changing at all is not true and, once in a while, will need to be swapped out.

- Roots on a raised bed garden tend to dry out quickly and the increased drainage also lends itself to the soil drying out a lot quicker than on conventional gardens. This requires garden enthusiasts to tend to the garden using complicated irrigation systems, particularly in the summer months when the climate is so warm that it tends to dry out the soil and can be detrimental to the plants.

Despite all this, know that the ease with which gardening can be done on a raised bed will still offer a lot of advantages.

It may be more expensive to start your raised garden and it may take more effort than, say, simply starting a conventional garden row in your own garden, but the effort does pay off.

Plants That Work Well In Raised Beds

Raised bed gardening is becoming more and more popular in order to take maximum advantage of small spaces. If you plant your raised bed garden correctly, you can get amazing crops of vegetables, flowers, and herbs with very little effort compared to what you must do in traditional gardening.

These types of gardens have an important role in the landscape of the home. They feature framed areas above the ground, and often have wooden frames around the area. They have an increased ability to drain away excess water, and eliminate compacted soil. In addition, you can add soil nutrients as necessary to help your plants be the best they can be. This allows gardeners to plant a variety of plants in their garden.

Most plants will work well in raised bed gardens. The exception is those plants that are large or have very deep roots or sprawling top growth. Other plants that don't work in raised beds are those that are top-heavy and tall and therefore need to be firmly anchored.

Since the plants in your raised beds will be sharing soil, light, fertilizer, and water, you should make sure to choose plants with similar or the same requirements for growth and development.

As far as size, moderately tall plants work well. Also, trailing plants or smaller plants work quite well in raised bed gardens, and can be planted together. Planting in raised beds is just another type of container gardening, and therefore basically requires you to follow the same rules. Plant your tallest plants in the center of your bed, and go down to the smaller plants near the edge. Plant the trailing plants along the edges, so they spill over.

Vegetables are pretty easy to grow in raised beds. You can maximize the amount of yield you get from your crops by planting the summer plants as soon as the spring ones have been harvested and fall ones as soon as the summer ones have been harvested. Since the fertilizer and soil are easier to control, you can plant vegetables and plants closer together than in a traditional garden.

In addition, raised bed gardens are being used to raise tropical houseplants as annuals. In the fall, you can dig them up and bring them in for the winter. The raised garden beds can be a spectacular addition to your backyard décor.

As far as flowering plants go, you can raise both annuals and perennials in your raised garden. You should choose annuals that match the availability of sunlight in your area. Annuals will add a pop of color and look great as border additions in your garden. The growing conditions offered in the raised bed garden seriously increase the growth of the annuals, so make sure that you allow enough room for them to grow. Annuals will flourish in the rich soil offered in the raised bed garden.

Perennials will give your garden a more permanent addition. They will flower year after year and can form the basis for your raised bed garden. You can add perennials to create a low maintenance garden that requires very little work through the seasons. To achieve constant color and flowering, you should choose plants that bloom at various times of the year.

Raised bed gardens are great for vegetable gardening because they offer a neat area for planting. The rich soil will ensure that you have a prosperous harvest, providing that you have placed them in such a way that there is room for growth. Make sure that you read all your labels so that you can decide on the best placement for the plants. An added benefit of the raised bed garden is that it keeps pests out- the frame provides a base to which you can place poles to attach fencing.

Peas

Peas work well in raised garden beds, according to the National Gardening Association. The raised design helps drain the excess water away and allows gardeners to plant earlier. You should plant peas after the last frost of the winter.

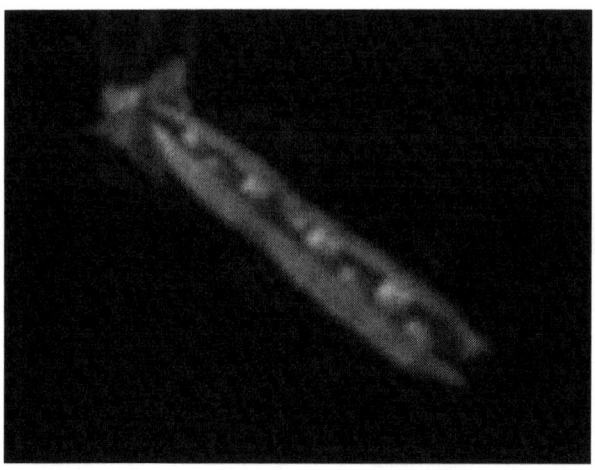

Peppers

According to the National Gardening Association, peppers grow quite well in raised bed gardens, especially if they're really wet. This is because of the drainage and the warmer temperatures offered by raised bed gardens. It's best to plant them after the last spring frost, but they can be started inside earlier and then moved outside in order to create an earlier harvest.

Eggplant

Like peppers, raised beds are great for growing eggplants. They like lots of sun as they grow and will do exceptionally well with a layer of mulch around the base of the plants in order to prevent the growth of weeds. Eggplants have beautiful purple flowers that make your vegetable garden especially attractive.

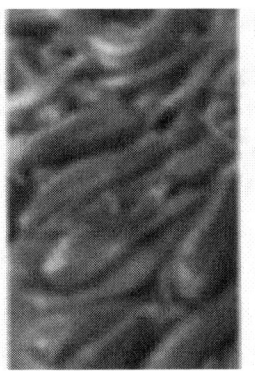

Okra

Okra grows quite well in raised beds and does really well next to peppers and eggplants. According to the National Gardening Association, you should plant okra from a seed. It doesn't do well with frost and doesn't do well in a really hot climate either. If you live in an area with a really cold winter, you can still plant okra, provided that your spring and summer months will be warm.

Another great addition to raised bed gardens are herbs. They grow just as well as the vegetables and annuals will. The extra organic material and the soil looseness allows the roots to spread quite nicely. When the roots spread, the plant can better absorb nutrients and moisture from the soil. Herbs can be paired with vegetables or annuals, or can be planted all on their own. You should disperse those strong-smelling herbs throughout the garden to repel insects. In addition, you will attract bees and butterflies, which will keep the pests to a minimal level.

Soil

Soil quality is as important to the quality of your raised-bed garden as sunlight and water. Soil that does not have the nutrients your plants need or that is too acidic or too alkaline will yield poor results. Soil drainage and density will also affect your results.

In this chapter, you will determine how much soil you need, what type is best, and where to get it as well as how to have your soil tested and how to interpret the findings.

Quality

One of the great features of raised-bed gardening is that you don't have to rely on your yard soil—you can fill your beds with a soil that meets your plants' temperature, water retention, mineral, nutrient, and other needs.

Soil doesn't just hold plant roots in place. It insulates them, keeping them at a relatively constant temperature during extreme weather conditions. Plants do not like sudden temperature changes.

Soil supplies water to plants. Water is an essential part of photosynthesis, the process by which plants feed themselves or create energy. Without photosynthesis, plants will die.

Soil provides minerals. You may have seen products marked "NPK," for nitrogen, phosphorus, and potassium, some of the most essential nutrients in gardening. Nitrogen promotes growth and leaf greening. Phosphorus allows plants to flower and fruit. Proper potassium levels lead to healthy roots, which help fight disease.

Soil also provides nutrients—a consideration in plant pairing (see here) and rotation (see here).

Topsoil—the top 2 to 8 inches of soil—contains the highest concentration of organic matter and nutrients, and, as you will learn in this chapter, it is the most desirable soil for raised beds (see here).

An important soil quality consideration is soil pH. On the pH scale of 0 to 14, a pH of 7 is neutral.

Any pH below 7 is acidic, and any pH above 7 is base, or alkaline. A good pH range for most garden vegetables is 6.1 to 6.9 (see here for how to measure pH). Some plants require more acidic soil, but they are not popular garden vegetables.

Another important soil quality consideration is soil density. Clay-filled soil is too compact for the roots of most flowers and vegetables to penetrate. Sandy soil is also not a good choice. It will not hold water. Most plants like fluffy soil that drains well.

To calculate how much soil you will need for your raised bed, use the example below for a 4-by-4-foot-by-6-inch bed.

Multiply the bed's width, length, and height in inches: 48 x 48 x 6 = 13,824.

If you want to know how many cubic feet of soil you need, divide the product above by 1,728

(number of cubic inches in a cubic foot): 13,824 ÷ 1,728 = 8.

If you want to know how many cubic yards of soil you need, divide the product by 46,656

(number of cubic inches in a cubic yard): 13,824 ÷ 46,656 = 0.29.

So, for our example, you need 8 cubic feet or 0.29 cubic yards of soil.

Mix

If you are on a tight budget, you can use topsoil from your yard, with the grass removed. Strain the soil through a screen and mix in compost equal to 25 percent of the topsoil. I do not recommend using your own yard's topsoil unless you have a budgetary issue. You will achieve better results with topsoil from a garden center or soil supplier.

Many nurseries sell a mix of topsoil and mulch by the truckload or the tractor bucket full. Nurseries typically sell the mixture they use for their own plants, so look around. If everything looks healthy, you will know you are getting a good mix. Discuss your needs with the nursery staff, who will be able to make recommendations.

To fill a small bed, you can purchase compost and topsoil in separate bags. Combine the contents on a tarp before transferring them to your bed. Don't combine the compost and topsoil in the bed.

Doing so won't result in a good mix, and it might require you to step into the bed, which would compact the soil.

Seasoned gardeners develop their own combinations of peat moss, pumice, vermiculite, compost, sand, shredded bark, cow manure, lime, fertilizer, and so on. I caution novice gardeners against creating their own soil combinations. The results could be far from ideal, adversely affecting plants.

If you really want to try a homemade soil mixture, use this foolproof formula: Combine equal parts peat moss, vermiculite, and compost in a clean trash can (so you have a container to store any excess).

Maintenance

You cannot fill your bed with soil once and forget it. Soil maintenance is an ongoing process. Your garden should always be kept clean. Any debris, such as dead leaves or overripe vegetables, should be removed to discourage disease and pests. Check for wilting, brown edges, holes in the leaves, and yellowing of your plants—all signs of a problem. Check under the leaves for bugs. If you find any, remove and dispose of them. If they are too small to remove, identify them and use an insecticidal soap. If you are unable to identify the bugs on your own, ask for help from your local extension agent (see Resources for information on how to find an agent near you).

You should also start a compost pile or find a good local compost source, then add compost to your garden every fall or early spring.

Overfilling your bed will cause some soil to run out on rainy days. Depressions in the soil surface will end up holding water. Check for problems on a regular basis and always after a heavy rain. You may need to level the soil surface, especially after plantings.

When filling your bed, mound the soil slightly so it forms a shallow slope to the bed's sides. Because the dirt will settle, you will occasionally need to add more of it to your bed. Be especially sure to check your soil surface between seasons. Maintenance is easier when a bed is not planted.

Check the pH of your soil by purchasing a soil pH meter, available at nurseries, big box stores, and online retailers for $10 to $30. The meter will tell you whether your soil is too acidic or alkaline. Most pH meters include a manual with information on identifying and correcting problems.

A soil moisture meter alerts you to overwatering. It can be found at nurseries, big box stores, and online retailers, and it costs $10 to $30. If you can't find a moisture meter, stick your finger into the soil about 2 inches deep. If it is dry to that point, you should water more. If it is soggy, you are overwatering.

Kits for testing your soil's NPK (nitrogen, potassium, and phosphorus) cost about $25 and let you know if you need to add fertilizer. Look for these kits at nurseries, big box stores, and online retailers. If your plants are healthy, and you are happy with them, you may never need to use one of these kits. But it never hurts to know exactly what is going on in your garden. You may identify one change that makes a big improvement.

Other maintenance tasks are weeding; staking or trellising plants that require it; and adding mulch, such as straw or bark chips, to your garden to help retain moisture around your plants and deter weeds.

A garden is truly a work of joy. Most gardeners find that going out every day and doing a quick once-over is not a chore, but rather the most enjoyable time of the day—especially if they find something to pick and eat!

How to test your Soil

Testing your soil is a good idea for first-time gardeners. It's the only way to know your soil's makeup. Is it too acidic or too alkaline? Does it have enough nitrogen, phosphorus, and potassium?

The best and easiest time to amend the soil is before you plant your garden. But because your garden is always changing, regularly testing and amending it is never a bad idea.

Aside from those kits that test soil moisture, pH, and NPK levels, the easiest and least expensive way to learn about your soil is to contact your local extension office (see here). Tell the agent the crops you are going to plant and request a soil testing. (My last soil testing cost about $15.) You will be given instructions on how to collect and mail a soil sample. Within a couple of weeks, you should receive a report identifying soil deficiencies and needed changes as well as instructions for making those changes.

Raised Beds: Site Preparation

One of the questions most frequently asked about raised beds for growing vegetables is just how tall they should be. There is no definite answer to this question, I am afraid. There is no 'ideal height'; it is completely up the individual. However, there are certain considerations that you must keep in mind. These include the soil conditions under the beds, the costs involved, the depth of the soil required for your specific crop and of course, which height would allow you to work comfortably in your raised beds. This last aspect should take priority if you are a matured gardener.

Preparation of the Ground

Double Dig

Although the plants in your raised beds will be provided with their own rich soil, some of them may grow roots that extend into the soil underneath the beds to search for additional nutrients and moisture. Therefore, it is important to prepare the soil below by double digging it. This must be done before you start on your raised beds and once done, need not be repeated.

Double digging simply means the depth to which you have to dig up the soil; it is approximately twenty-four inches deep, or in other words, two lengths of the blade of your shovel. Remove all the hard rocks and debris that could obstruct roots from growing down into the ground. Keep your eyes open for other large roots entering into this space. For instance, trees that grow nearby can send their roots to more than fifty feet diagonally underneath the surface searching for nutrients and water. Double digging will provide an extended reservoir of water and nutrients, which your plants' sturdier, deeper roots can have access to.

Digging up the ground also allows you to have a closer look at the status of the underlying soil, and to decide which amendments should be made. If it resembles clay, for instance, peat should be used to lighten it in order to aerate it and improve the drainage.

Improving the Subsoil

You have cleared the ground area of debris and rock and finished your double digging. If needed, you can now add some peat moss that will lighten your soil. Because peat has an acidic nature, you have to balance the pH level of the soil by adding lime. Sprinkle some rock phosphate over the plot and mix in with the soil. Your ground area is now ready for the raised plant bed, so assemble the frames and fill up with rich soil. When you almost reach the top of the raised bed, add compost and fertilizer. Do not add the compost and fertilizer too long before the season to avoid early, unexpected spring rainfalls to flush them too far down into your soil.

Ideal Height for Raised Beds

Consider Drainage

Raised beds have an aesthetic appeal, which speaks to many gardeners, but they also allow for proper drainage of the soil in which your veggies will be grown. In general, most raised beds are eleven inches tall, which is equal to that of two 2 by 6 standard boards. (In actual fact the measurements are 1.5 by 5.5 inches.) The reason why this height is most popular is that it provides adequate drainage for the majority of crops. The best results can be achieved if you allow for another twelve inches at least of rich soil underneath your raised bed. That will give your veggie plants up to twenty inches of good soil. Remember that raised beds usually end up not filled to the brim with soil; after every watering the soil will compress somewhat. You will need this extra space later to add some mulch.

Two factors contribute to the earlier warming up of the soil in raised beds during the spring: Firstly, the soil is always well above the ground level and the second aspect is the good drainage in these beds. Gardeners can, therefore, start transplanting much earlier and so lengthen the growing season of their veggies. To shield the young, vulnerable seedlings from a late frost or strong winds, place cold frames over the beds. Once the seedlings are stronger and better established, these frames can simply be removed and used elsewhere if needed.

Consider Bending Down

Young gardeners who are fit and energetic might not even waste time thinking about this aspect since going on your knees or bending down to attend to your plants is easy and you take it in your stride. People who suffer from backache or strain, or those whose mobility have been impaired will need higher raised beds to help lighten their gardening chores. Beds can be in a range of eight to twenty four inches high. You will quickly notice the huge difference between tending these various beds. Taller beds are just so much more comfortable when you have to set in transplants, till the soil, weed and harvest. It is not necessary to put extras strain on your back at all.

Cross Supports for Taller Beds

It is commonsense that taller beds will hold more volume so you have to keep this in mind when you construct a raised bed that is taller than twelve inches, (especially if it is longer than five feet). As mentioned before, after a few watering, the soil will compact slightly, becoming heavier and the pressure may well cause your beds to bulge out on the sides in mid-span. So for beds of this height you will require cross supports. Place them in the middle of the span, right across the width. This will prevent the two sides from bulging out. If you purchased your raised beds from a garden center these supports were probably included in the package but if your raised beds are home-made, you will have to make your own, using composite plastic, aluminum or wood.

Soil Depth for Most Vegetables

The Roots Need Adequate Depth

Most nutrients in garden beds are to be found in the top six inches of the soil. The reason is that most vegetable root growth happens in this shallow depth. The key nutrients like fertilizers and compost are added from the top and then tilled in lightly. Mulches also are applied on the top surfaces of the beds from time to time; they eventually decompose to add extra nutrients to the soil, enriching it.

If moisture and nutrients are available deeper in the soil, tap roots will grow down to reach them. This brings additional trace minerals to the vegetable plants as well. The larger the plant, the deeper the roots will travel. Deeper roots anchor the plant much firmer into the bed, enabling it to withstand strong winds or heavy rains and saturated soil. Plants with big leaves and shallow root systems like broccoli, cauliflower and Brussels sprouts will need staking to make sure they do not fall over as they develop and reach maturity.

Raised beds which have been set on a gravel surface or a concrete patio will not allow roots to grow any deeper down than the depth of the beds. In this case, make sure you know the depth requirements for the different crops. You can compensate for an impenetrable ground surface by making the beds higher, providing enough root space.

The average raised bed is between eight and twelve inches tall, but experienced gardeners have planted in beds with sides exceeding three feet. While these beds are ideal for crops with deep roots, you have to provide good drainage by drilling a number of holes towards the bottom of your beds, right along the sides.

Soil Preparation

Every successful gardener will tell you that soil preparation comes first when you aim for a bountiful harvest. Without proper soil, you may as well throw in the towel before you even begin. Initially you should focus all your attention on the condition and quality of soil you are going to use. A good quality soil will ensure that your vegetable plants grow to their full potential and that you will not spend too much valuable time fighting pests and weeds.

Following are a few tips for mixing rich and fertile soil to suit all your planters and garden beds. Your locality may influence the type of soil you will need to a small degree, but these basic principles are applicable everywhere, regardless of where you live.

1. Topsoil does not Always Contain Organic Matter

Purchased soil often looks quite promising: dark in color, well screened and clean. This might not always be an indication of what it actually contains. It may well be a good growing medium though without any of the vital organic matter that is essential for growth. Therefore, you should always inquire from the attendant at the garden center what the soil consists of and what its origin is. You should assume that some extra feeding would be necessary to build up this soil to the standards needed for successful gardening.

2.   Revitalize Soil Annually

Usually new gardens will do fairly well during their initial year even though no additional matter was added to amend the soil. The reason for this is that the available nutrients, organic matter and trace minerals have not been tapped yet. However, after one or two seasons of successive gardening, the crops will have used up all the riches in the soil. That is why it is so important that you revitalize your gardening soil regularly.

A wonderful solution is to plant 'green manure' as a cover crop after the first two seasons of growing vegetables. These crops are very easy and simple to grow and have many benefits. As soon as the cover crop has matured, chop it up and then dig it lightly into your soil. Now your soil has been replenished with fresh organic matter. Consider growing leguminous crops like alfalfa or fenugreek since they will fix the atmospheric nitrogen in such a way that it can be used as nutrients by the plants. This type of green manure has many benefits; their roots will loosen the soil, bringing the deeper nutrients nearer to the surface of your garden beds. While you chop up the manure and work it into the ground as well as the activity of the roots will aerate your soil, thus improving the drainage for future crops.

3. Soil must be Crumbly, Fluffy and Light

You want to make it as easy as possible for the roots of your plants to be able to work their way through the layers of soil in search of moisture and nutrients. Compacted and dense soil will make this essential task of plant roots very difficult and they will spend so much energy struggling to get to the nutrients that not much will be left for the rest of the plant to grow. You can easily facilitate better root growth by lightening your garden soil. This is turn will lead to better vegetative growth and you will see the positive results when your plants start to flourish.

4.   The Ultimate Amendment for Soil: Compost

Making your own compost is easy and can save you extra expenses. Many gardeners have a compost heap in their back gardens. Compost consists of organic material filled with nutrients to turn normal soil into a rich medium for all your plants.   Use this valuable resource correctly and wisely and you can be sure of a prolific vegetable garden. Instead of adding compost to the soil right after harvesting, rather postpone it to two or three weeks before you plant your next crop. You want to prevent a sudden downpour from washing away all that wonderful richness in the compost and undo all your hard work.

5.   Organic Fertilizers are the Best Choice

Do not be overly enticed by all the many product claims you read on the packaging of chemical fertilizers. They may be true, but the advantages often do not last and are rather short-lived. You will have to reapply them regularly after each planting. In the end, the benefits of these commercial fertilizers may be lessened to some extend because they do not improve the condition of the soil, the most important aspect of successful gardening.

6.   Rock Phosphate

If you a new gardener, using the plot or raised bed for the first time, you will probably be able to use the basic soil for one or two years. After this, you will have to add some source of phosphorus to it. Your crops will grow steadily and vigorously and mature early because of the addition of this element. You will have larger-sized vegetables and fruit in autumn. Crops, which mature earlier, will better avoid summer drought and be less vulnerable to disease and frost. Rock phosphate also contains a number of minor elements like zinc, boron, iodine and nickel, all necessary in smaller doses for plants to grow optimally. Furthermore, rock phosphate works long-term, thus releases its elements slowly so that the plant will benefit over a longer period.

Pest Control

Pests are a staple of gardens or farms, and your raised bed will not be an exception. All you can do is just to get yourself prepared for them whenever they decide to manifest themselves. You should be more careful and take preventive measures especially if you want to grow delicious fruits or fresh vegetables. These are the kind of plants that pests are most attracted to.

You can apply some chemical controls to do away with the invasion of these pests, some of them which are very effective. But there are some other non-chemical methods of pest control that you can employ to control pest, most of which won't have any side effects on the garden.

Here are some of the most common pest that attack gardens

1. Slugs

These pests are very slow but steady vegetable 'munchers', and if care is not taken, the entire crop can be wiped out in a few nights. The elevation that comes with raised beds will mean that fewer of these slugs will be able to find their way to the garden, but this does not entirely stop them.

Slugs are naturally slow pests and you can easily spot some of them lying at the base of the raised bed trying to get to the top of the garden. You can pick them up and dispose them however that fits you.

There are two non-chemical methods I employ to help me with slug control. The first is to make a beer or sugary solution trap. Slugs are attracted to that kind of thing. Place the solution in a container that has been sunk into the ground so that the top is level with the ground. Slugs will gather into the container and feed on the solution and they will be unable to get out until you arrive.

The second is to scatter orange peels around the bases of the garden to attract them. Then you come and pick them up and dispose.

2. Birds

Birds play an important role in protecting the garden from the invasion of pest, but nevertheless, they still take out them to consume some of the plants whenever they can. For example, pigeons are known to love cabbages and sprouts. Most other birds will love to devour some ripe fruits.

One way to keep your plants secured and protected from birds is to protect them with a bird net and using a raised bed makes it easier construct. You can make a protective cage by simply digging in some bamboo sticks into the ground around the raised bed. Then use a net to cover it until every part of the bed has been protected.

3. Aphids

They can be found on the shoot and leaves of plants. One way in which I control their invasion is by releasing ladybug or lacewing larvae around the plants that they have attacked. The larvae feed on the aphids.

4. Carrot Fly

These flies are particularly attracted to the smell of carrot. You can prevent their attack by growing resistant carrot species or cover the growing carrot with a fine mesh to keep off the tiny flies.

5. Beetles

They can feed on your plants no matter how small and immature they are. You can make use of Milky spore to eliminate the grubs (their larvae form).

6. Rodents

These ones feed on the seeds you have just planted out, mostly peas or beans. They also won't hesitate to feed on fruits and corn seeds.

You can get rids of them by covering the raised bed with wire nets or by making use of poisons. Consult your local pest control company for the best rodent poison that won't affect the plants.

One of the things that mixed planting is good for is pest control, as we have mentioned the combination of different plants can confuse the pests and help control their breeding program. However there are certain plants that you do not want to mix together because they encourage the same pest. This could lead to an exacerbation of your pest problems, instead of the opposite.

For instance, if you consider pest control to be a major objective in your growing regime, it is not wise to grow sweetcorn and tomatoes together as they both attract the corn ear-worm, also known as the tomato fruit worm. Tomatoes, eggplant, peppers and potatoes are a favourite of the Colorado beetle; while squash, melons and cucumbers are a favourite snack for the pickleworm.

Pest control in a raised bed

Controlling slugs in a raised bed situation is particularly easy, compared to the traditional growing methods. Simply fix some copper tape around the edge of the raised bed; slugs will not cross copper as it has a chemical reaction to their slime. Copper paint will do as well.

There are of course the usual tips about beer traps or bran and vinegar to attract them. Either method works by setting a trap including these ingredients and hiding it under a roof tile or similar. The slugs are attracted to the traps where they can then be disposed of.

Carrot fly prevention is one of the bonuses of a raised bed as carrot fly do not tend to go over 18 inches or so, as a general rule. This means that the higher raised beds have a good advantage over the battle with carrot fly. One of the top tips to keep away the carrot fly include extending your raised bed frame height by about one foot or so, then adding some fine insect mesh around it.

This can be very effective against the carrot fly, as they are low flyers as mentioned, and so this will prevent them from dropping by and laying their eggs on your young carrots.

In general however the advantage of the raised bed, is that it is fairly easy, especially if you have developed the cold-frame idea, to flip a fine nylon mesh over your crop. This will prevent the egg-laying butterflies and moths from getting access.
It will also prevent the birds from helping themselves either to the young seedling or indeed your strawberry harvest.

Methods Of Raised Bed Gardening

There are also different methods that are used in Raised Bed Gardening and it will be helpful for you to get acquainted with them. Take note that different methods work for different plants and that you can always choose the one you're comfortable with—and the one you know will work for what you have in your garden.

Intensive Gardening

Intensive Gardening is said to be one of the most successful methods used in raised bed gardening. It has also been around for thousands of years now because even early horticulturists have been doing this method for years.

Basically, what happens is that there is close spacing between plants in garden beds so that the soil will stay fertile, and succession planting can easily be done. It's also said to be great for maximizing available gardening space, which can bring you 4 to 10 times more harvest than other types of methods.

Scheduling, planning, and time are all important if you want this method to work, so you have to start gradually and make it a part of your daily habit. In short, consistency is key. The best way to do this is by building at least two raised beds for each gardening season. For this method, green manure and cover crops prove to be extremely helpful.

Lasagna Gardening

For this type of gardening, tilling won't need to be done. It's almost the same as using composting sheets, so you can easily take off weeds and grass away from your plants. Lasagna beds can also easily be placed on top of existing beds—thus the name.

What's great about lasagna gardens is that you can create them during any season. However, you have to add extra compost and topsoil during the spring and summer seasons. 2 to 3 inches of each will do—which is also the same amount that you should use for perennial crops.

What you have to do is cut the grass extremely short at ground level so that you can easily scalp seeds. Then, use around 6 to 10 pieces of newspaper to cover the bed above the vegetation that's originally there. If you don't like to use newspapers, you can also use flattened cardboard boxes—just make sure to wet them. You can also add mulch over the soil—handful by handful until you have covered the bed. For overlaps, use newspapers or cardboard. The important thing is to make sure that everything has been properly covered.

Now, you can layer organic matter on top of the mulch. Mix brown and green manure together to create compost and then add weeds (without the roots), sawdust, used potting soil, garden trimmings, and newspaper. Chopped leaves can be used, too. Then, cover them with topsoil but make sure to leave a 1-inch pile for the mulch, and just wait for them to decompose in a few months.

Succession Planting

For this method, what you have to do is make sure that after harvesting crops, you go on and plant new ones on the same space. It maximizes soil fertility and space, as well, and will bring rapid growth of the plants. Most gardeners and farmers do this, especially when they're in that line of business.

To make it work, you have to plant warm season vegetables in place of cool season ones. For example, after harvesting spinach or peas, you can then plant squash or beans in their place—perfect for the next season! Now, once you have harvested these beans, you can then replace them with spinach and vice versa. It's a cycle that you have to maintain all throughout the year.

You can also try giving 1 to 2 week intervals in between planting so that the harvest period can be prolonged, and so that you can also plant mid-season vegetables—so the cycle will be maximized, and once you have harvested them, you can replace them at least 4 times in just one year!

Close Plant Spacing

Another thing that you can do is close plant spacing, which is said to yield some of the best results. This is because crop production is intensified by at least 80% when there are closed spaces and pathways between the crops.

You can place plants close together in a staggered or triangular pattern so that the maturity won't be overlapped and so that the leaf canopies can protect the plants and the beds from too much sunlight. Doing this will also kill weeds, conserve moisture, and moderate the temperature of the soil.

Remember to plan each planting session as carefully as you can and make sure to add green manure sometime during the year. Watering is essential in this type of setting, too.

A Few Reminders for a successful application of Raised Bed Gardening Methods

Have them face south

One of the best tips that one should never forget is to make sure that you lay out the beds horizontally so they can face the south of the garden. It will work best if the longest beds are the ones closest to the south.

The reason why this needs to be done is to make sure that all of the plants in the garden will receive the proper—and equal amount of lighting. However, by letting the end parts of the beds face the south, you are also limiting your chances of planting more crops, especially when variety is concerned. It will also limit sunlight from reaching small plants at the back. If you can remember, it is said that it's best to plant the tall plants at the back so that the small ones can get sunlight without any blockage.

A balanced diet

Plants need to have a great diet, too! Look for organic fertilizers and make sure that you use certain types of soil amendments that contain the following: Nitrogen, which is usually found in alfalfa meals, composted manure, and cover crops; Magnesium, which raises PH levels so plants won't dry up, and which can be found in Epsom salts;

Calcium, just like people, plants also need calcium to grow strong. Calcium is usually found in lime or gypsum and provides nutrients most especially for acidic soil;

Potassium, which can be found in greensand or kelp meal;

Phosphorus, which can be found in rock phosphate and bone meal, and;

Sulfur, but only if you're using Alkaline soil and if you need to lower PH levels of extremely acidic plants.

Providing your plants with these nutrients will make you breathe a sigh of relief as it's a sign that nutrient deficiency will be blocked.

Keep those pests away

Pests will do nothing good to your plants and one easy way to keep them away is by making sure that you lay galvanized mesh or hardware cloth across the bottom of the soil once it's on the bed already. Use ½ or ¼" layer of the said mesh cloth, and make sure that it continues up to 3" from where it was first laid on.

However, if you're trying to grow carrots, potatoes, and root crops, you have to remember to set the mesh as low as possible or just choose to buy raised garden planters in place of them. These would keep those crops safe.

Mulch between beds

Keep in mind that you should keep a perforated layer of landscape cloth on top of the soil when you are trying to weed out the pathways. Use 2 to 3" of coarse sawdust or bark mulch to cover this and let it reach up to 1" of the bottom of the bed. After that, you can then staple it to the bed so you won't have to mulch over and over again. Don't worry about esthetics because mulch will already be able to cover this.

Spread out the soil

By spreading out the soil, you can be sure that every plant you put in there will be able to receive equal amounts of nutrients, water, and sunlight. Of course, you can never be too sure about how equal it is, so you'd just have to add soil amendments, such as lime, compost, or peat and then top it off with topsoil. This way, they can all come together and eventually, you'll notice that they've all been spread out evenly!

Bed Leveling

It may be a bit meticulous to use bed levels but it will keep those beds safer, which in turn could lengthen their life. This way, you'll be able to use them more in years to come. What you have to do is put a 2 x 4" board on each side of the bed and tap the sides down until you reach the size that you desire.

Root Check

Don't forget to check for roots coming from other plants that may snatch the nutrients that are meant for the plants in your bed. When you see one, pull it out right away. Never ever allow the roots to grow. You can also install a root barrier.

Conclusion

Starting a raised bed garden is a great way to accommodate that budding little gardener in your family. It is the ideal way for kids to learn about nature; they will see the wonder of a little seedling emerging from the ground, growing tiny leaves and later develop into a mature plant with fruit. Planting in raised beds will make it convenient for both you and the young ones to reach every plant in the box without ending up with muddy feet or knees full of dirt.

Now that you have all the information needed, it is time to get going. Walk around your available space during the day to find a sunny location. Once you have decided where you want to place your raised bed, decide on the size and dimensions. The next step is to make a list of everything you will need, from the soil, compost and other materials, to the frames. Once your bed is up and filled up with the soil mixture, it is time to turn your attention to the plants. Select the type of veggies you want to grow according to the guidelines I have provided. If you want to grow plants from seeds, you will have to do some prior planning since it will take time for them to develop into seedlings ready to be planted outside in your box. Otherwise, you can purchase seedlings to plant directly into your raised beds.

Now most of the work is done and the fun part starts. While you wait for your veggies to grow, a little attention is needed; water them regularly and keep your eyes peeled for any pests or weeds. Then wait for the fruit to mature and start harvesting!

Growing vegetables in raised beds makes gardening a pleasure. With limited time and space, you can grow an abundance of food in a small area. The benefits are numerous; fewer weeds and pests, better drainage, better soil, no compacting of the soil, less pain potential for you, the gardener, to name but a few. Your friends will envy your neat, attractive garden and harvest of healthy, tasty vegetables. If there was ever any need for gardening enthusiasts to exercise creativity and their building know-how in the garden, there's nothing like taking on raised bed gardening as a project to prove it.

From its more obvious advantages such as soil control, easy pest management and overall ease when it comes to maintenance, it's also ideal for anyone with physical disabilities and limitations, as it provides better access for your garden without requiring you to put a strain on your back. In terms of water, it is actually easier to maintain and set up an irrigation system for raised gardens. And if you have pets, you can rest assured that they won't be messing up your garden, as it will be harder for them to get to it.

Printed in Poland
by Amazon Fulfillment
Poland Sp. z o.o., Wrocław

57383261R00094